Super-stitions

1,013 of the Wackiest Myths, Fables & Old Wives' Tales

DEBORAH MURRELL

Reader's Digest

The Reader's Digest Association, Inc.
Pleasantville, NY/Montreal/Sydney/London/Singapore

A READER'S DIGEST BOOK

This edition published by The Reader's Digest Association, Inc., by arrangement with Amber Books Ltd.

Copyright © 2008 Amber Books Ltd.

Produced by Amber Books Ltd.
Bradley's Close
74–77 White Lion Street
London N1 9PF

FOR AMBER BOOKS

Project Editor James Bennett
Design Manager Mark Batley
Copy Editing Constance Novis, Siobhan O'Connor
Illustrations Ray & Corinne Burrows (Beehive Illustration)

FOR READER'S DIGEST

U.S. Project Editor Kimberly Casey
Copy Editors Amy Boaz, Mary Connell, Barbara McIntosh Webb
Canadian Project Editor Pamela Johnson
Project Designer Jennifer Tokarski
Senior Art Director George McKeon
Executive Editor, Trade Publishing Dolores York
Associate Publisher Rosanne McManus
President and Publisher, Trade Publishing Harold Clarke

Library of Congress Cataloging-in-Publication Data

Murrell, Deborah Jane, 1963–
  Superstitions : 1,013 of the world's wackiest myths, fables & old wives tales / Deborah Murrell.
      p. cm.
  Includes index.
  ISBN 978-0-7621-0922-7
1. Superstition. I. Title.
  BF1775.M87 2008
  001.9'6--dc22

                                          2008016894

We are committed to both the quality of our products and the service we provide to our customers.
We value your comments, so please feel free to contact us.

            The Reader's Digest Association, Inc.
            Adult Trade Publishing
            Reader's Digest Road
            Pleasantville, NY 10570-7000

For more Reader's Digest products and information, visit our website:
            www.rd.com (in the United States)
            www.readersdigest.ca (in Canada)
            www.rdasia.com (in Asia)
            www.readersdigest.co.uk (in the UK)
            www.readersdigest.com.au (in Australia)
            www.readersdigest.com.nz (in New Zealand)

Printed in China

10 9 8 7 6 5 4 3 2 1

Contents

Introduction   7

Hearth & Home   12

Sickness & Health   32

Love & Romance   52

Engagement & Marriage   70

Fertility   88

Babies & Children   98

Success & Wealth   114

Spirits & Souls   132

Magical Little People   148

Omens   164

Good Luck Charms   186

Protective Amulets   200

Numbers   216

Calendar Customs & Rituals   230

Index   248

Introduction

Have you ever stopped to think about why people refuse to walk under ladders? Or say "God bless you!" when someone sneezes? Or stop to pick up a "lucky" penny? Superstitions stem from ancient fears and beliefs, and help society cope with the unexplainable. In earlier times, few people could read or write, but they were steeped in mythology and folklore. They invoked superstitions as a way of making sense of the world around them.

Controlling Your Destiny

Natural phenomena, weather, and other inexplicable occurrences like death gave rise to a deep-seated belief in omens. The force of fate ruled the world; and by following a particular action—such as protecting your home by keeping clover inside, planting crops during certain phases of the moon to enhance fertility, or not getting married on a Friday—you could increase your chances for prosperity and good luck. Carrying a rabbit's foot or a horseshoe were traditional ways of inviting good luck, and they helped the wearer feel that he had some control over his destiny.

Thanks to modern science, many of these superstitions no longer hold—or do they?

The causes of weather, natural phenomena, and disease have been explained by science, and the superstitions surrounding them—such as the ominous passing of a comet, or the questionable "cures" given to sick people—are no longer relevant. However, many superstitions still persist, even if there isn't a majority belief in them. Who doesn't sometimes get a shiver down the spine when a black cat crosses his path, or feel uneasy when a dog howls in the middle of the night? People may be less superstitious today than they were in previous ages. Yet even the most diehard rationalists still use language that relates to superstition. Without even thinking you might say "break a leg" to an actor to wish him a successful performance, or you "knock on wood" to bring about a good outcome—and stave off the "bad karma" or punishment that may ensue. That's the thing about superstitions: They can be so ingrained in our psyches that they are part of our unconscious lives. We almost can't help invoking them, whether we believe in them or not.

These ancient practices were probably passed along orally, guarded during the period known in Europe as the Dark Ages, then rekindled and transformed in the late Middle Ages or Renaissance, when the Christian Church came to dominate the West. Religious leaders of any kind were unlikely to encourage superstitions, since many of them contradicted the teachings of the faith, in whatever religious community one might have lived. However, many superstitions actually arose out of religious beliefs, and were even promulgated by the clergy. Some Christian priests, for example, allowed the stubs of consecrated candles to be taken by parishioners for use as protection from evil spirits. Others performed exorcisms against witchcraft or "possession" by the devil.

In ancient times, the origins of the world—its mysterious functioning

> "If a black cat walks in my path, I will immediately turn around and go home, even if I am on my way somewhere."
>
> —Hip-hop recording artist Missy Elliott

Origins of Superstitions

We often think that superstitions are primitive beliefs, dating back to classical Greek or Roman times, ancient Egypt, or even earlier. Some of them probably do, although it is unlikely that they have survived continuously in the meantime.

present and future—were explained by mythology and folklore. Religion came to provide the same purpose, and its believers are often susceptible to superstition. However, they are not the only ones. Many people who do not believe in a supreme deity perform rituals and rites based on superstitious beliefs. Consider, for example, people who pursue careers where luck can play a significant part. These include the armed forces, theater, fire fighting, and sports, to name just a few.

It would be fair to say that most of the beliefs considered superstitious are

We now know how lightning occurs, although people in ages past might have understood the rudiments of electricity by the English custom of covering reflective surfaces during a storm. In folklore, circles of mushrooms in woodland glades were "fairy rings," caused by fairies dancing at night. In fact, fairy rings are

"Superstition is the poetry of life."

—German poet, novelist, and playwright Johann Wolfgang von Goethe, 1819

irrational and have no basis in reality. Many superstitions come from a time when there was little knowledge or understanding of the ways of the world, nature, or the universe. Yet given the acceptance of the validity of recent science, humanity continues to hang on to traditional beliefs and practices. Why, we might wonder, would a person think that daisy petals could predict whether or not someone might find him or her attractive? Why should an apple peel thrown over a shoulder form itself into the shape of the initial letter of a future lover? Or why would a bird perching on a house or tapping at its windows have any significance at all? These superstitions seem to have an ability to grip the human imagination in a way that science does not.

Science and Philosophy

Modern science can explain many things for us that our ancestors might have reasoned away with folklore and myth.

made when an underground fungus sends threads called hyphae outward from a central point. Mushrooms are the fruiting body of the fungus, but these will not become visible until the season and weather are right, and then each of those mushrooms might spore and start the growth cycle of another ring. These magical patterns inspired all kinds of superstitions involving fairies, and you could even run around the rings for good luck—but not more than nine times!

Medicinal herbs and other plants are a familiar case in point. In the last few decades it was discovered that many traditional cures contain chemicals or compounds now known to be effective treatments for a variety of illnesses. For example, spiderwebs provided both a natural and

traditional remedy for a bleeding wound, and were very effective. Shakespeare—who chronicled, and therefore preserved many superstitions—mentions this ancient remedy, in the words of Bottom in *A Midsummer Night's Dream*:

I shall desire you of more acquaintance, good Master Cobweb; if I cut my finger I shall make bold with you.

Sometimes science and superstition meet happily somewhere in between, as in the fail-safe panacea administered in Tibet: When a doctor has run out of the medicine someone needs, he writes its name on paper and the patient swallows the paper instead. It is said to have the same effect as the medicine itself!

Egyptians, for whom the triangle was the perfect form. The Trinity was the ideal godhead not only for Christians, but for Hindus as well, and in Islam the worshipper was to make three pilgrimages, to Mecca, Medina, and Jerusalem. However, it's now commonly thought that bad luck comes in threes, and lighting three cigarettes from one match is said to be fatal.

Moreover, followers of Pythagoras believed that man was the equivalent of eight notes of a full musical chord and that God was the completing ninth component. Pliny the Elder, the Roman author of *Naturalis Historia*, recorded the belief that an odd number of eggs in a nest was the best assurance of hatching plenty of hen chickens rather than unproductive rooster chicks. By the late nineteenth century, the ideal number became 13 eggs, although that number began to plummet in popularity, as

"Superstition sets the world in flames; philosophy quenches them."

—French writer and philosopher Voltaire, 1764

Philosophers have also contributed to the stubborn perpetuation of many superstitions. Consider the many superstitions about numbers. The ancient Greek mathematician Pythagoras thought three was the perfect number; the symbol of a beginning, a middle, and an end, reflecting the similar conviction by the

evidenced by the dreaded 13th floor and Friday the 13th.

Types of Superstition
Many superstitions, especially today, are based on a straightforward belief in luck, or fate, as an actual force in the world. This force, in some cases, cannot be

avoided. But in others, it can be sidestepped by following a particular action or doing certain chores at the right time or day of the year.

If misfortune can't be averted, it might be nullified, by enacting some kind of ritual to appease the Fates. For example, according to a commonly held theater superstition, it is unlucky to whistle in a fertility, bearing and raising children, prosperity, and death—in the first eight chapters. These superstitions also include beliefs in magic, witchcraft, and other occult or supernatural powers. Chapter 9 is devoted to the otherworldly characters, such as fairies and elves, who crop up in superstitions as well as mythology and folklore tales around the world.

> "Most theatrical people are terribly conscious of what brings good and bad luck. For instance, you never quote from *Macbeth*. It's the unluckiest of plays, and every time there's a production, something happens."
>
> —Actress Diana Rigg

dressing room. If you do, you have to step outside, turn around three times and knock before walking back in.

Some superstitions can be grouped together into specific types. For example, beliefs based on "beginnings," such as the way a journey or effort begins will reflect on its end. So if a person, creature, or object considered unlucky is encountered at the start, the end will also be unfortunate. However, canceling your plans and starting over again can sometimes allay bad luck.

In this book, you'll find superstitions that relate to many aspects of human life—hearth and home, sickness and health, love and romance, betrothals and marriage, There are also superstitions that use talismans and amulets for protection from evil or to attract of good fortune. Omens, or events perceived as signs of events to come, warrant their own chapter, and so does the fascinating subject of numbers. Finally, the last chapter provides a look at the rituals around the world for "guaranteeing" a happy ending for the old year, and a favorable start to the new one.

Hearth
& Home

A place to live is the most significant and probably the most expensive purchase many of us will ever make, whether it is a mansion on a hill, a house in the suburbs, or an apartment in the middle of the city. Our home represents security and belonging, a place of shelter, so it is hardly surprising that most people protect their homes by buying insurance to pay for damage to the structure itself or to its contents. Still, there have always been those prepared to go one step further than the practical to guard against things going wrong and protect what is theirs. The superstitious have always had other ways of shielding their home from misfortune, bad luck, disease, and general calamity, and of attracting good luck and encouraging prosperity.

New Home, Old Tricks

Traditionally, there were superstitions for every nook and cranny of the home, and taking certain precautions or watching for omens was a way of life. Despite the way our homes and lifestyles have changed over the centuries, a surprising number of superstitions persist.

Moving to a New Home

When something begins well, it gives us confidence that things will continue that way. Beginnings are therefore often seen as significant in their own right. This belief makes superstitious people work hard to create good luck right from the outset of a new venture. As moving into a house or apartment marks a beginning, there are many superstitions surrounding the events involved in moving into a new home.

Some people believe that things beyond our control, such as the weather, can affect the future luck of a household. It is said to be bad luck to move on a rainy day, for example, yet there is little anyone can do to prevent rain. You can, however, avoid moving on a Friday, which is said to be an unfortunate day for many activities.

A woman planting lavender in the garden can bring bad luck on the household; always be sure that a man plants it instead.

Follow the Moon

You can also time your move so that it coincides with when the moon is waxing, rather than waning; the waxing of the moon appears in many superstitions, especially those connected with beginnings, as a positive time of the month.

Floor Plan

If you live in an apartment building, you should try to avoid moving to another apartment on a lower floor in the same building. This may be a superstitious way to prevent yourself from "going down in the world." You don't need to worry about this belief, however, when you are moving to a different building.

Coal, Bread, Salt...and a New Broom

When moving into a new home, it is often thought to be a good idea to take some staples of life with you, such as coal, bread, and salt. Coal signifies warmth, bread represents food, and salt has a number of practical uses. Salt is a mild antiseptic and a food preservative, but it also has a ritual significance as a purifier. So, for an auspicious start to life in a new home, salt is sprinkled in the hearths and the corners of every room in the house and sometimes specifically by children, presumably because they also symbolize purity.

In Scotland, as early as the sixteenth century, eggs laid on Ascension Day were hung in the roof as protection against "all hurts."

Other superstitions recommend bringing a loaf of bread and a new broom to your new home. The bread symbolizes food and plenty, but the broom is a symbol for sweeping out the old spirits or any bad luck left behind by the previous owners. Remember, though, that to bring good luck it must be a new broom, never an old one. This may be related to a belief that leaning a broom against a bed will cause evil spirits to leap from between its bristles and cast a spell on the bed. It was also believed that leaning a broom in a corner would bring strangers to the house—not always a good thing.

Carrying the Bride

Another very well known superstition involving beginnings is the tradition of carrying a bride over the threshold of her marital home, mentioned as far back as the first century by the Greek historian Plutarch. Whoever entered the home first would be the master of it, so carrying the bride over the threshold ensures that both parties enter the house at the same time and, therefore, creates an equal partnership in the home.

The elder tree has protective benefits against evil spirits and witches, but cutting, sawing, or tampering with elder in any way after dark will actually attract them.

Alternatively, it may be a tactic to prevent the woman from coming into contact with the evil spirits that often lurked under the threshold. It is also thought unlucky if the bride stumbles when entering her new home, and being carried definitely avoids that possibility, too. It seems unlikely that the tradition of carrying the bride over the threshold would have continued unbroken from Plutarch's time. It may have been rediscovered in classic literature, however, and the tradition was revived at some point since the Middle Ages.

Gifts for the New Home Owners

It is traditional for people visiting you for the first time in your new home to bring such gifts as coal, with its association with warmth. Coal is a favorite among the superstitious as a suitable gift. A knife, however, is frowned upon because it might "cut love," or cause a quarrel. If you do give someone a knife as a present, they must always gift you with a coin at the same time, to ensure that you do not "sever" the friendship.

Cats and the New Home

A tradition that originated in the United States is to put the family cat into the new house for the first time through the window rather than the door. This is said to prevent your beloved feline from running away. Another tactic is to butter the cat's paws, which usually has the effect of making it stay at least until it has licked them clean, by which time it has hopefully adjusted to its new home. In Ireland, a country seemingly steeped in ritual and superstition, up until the twentieth century, it was considered unlucky to take a cat from an old home to a new one. This tradition, sadly, probably resulted in many cats being turned out of their homes.

Locking Out Bad Luck

Planting for Protection

You can safeguard your home from various calamities, including storms, witchcraft, and vermin, by using plants.

- Plant garlic on the thatch over the door to ward off general unpleasantness and things that go bump in the night. Not moving into a thatched cottage? Don't panic. Instead, nail a branch of evergreen to new rafters once you have moved in, to bring good luck and protection.
- Houseleeks, or liveforever (*Sempervivum tectorum*), when planted on the walls and roof of a house, have been believed to protect against thunder and lightning since at least the middle of the sixteenth century. Houseleeks are still used in herbal remedies to cool fevers and burns, so it may be this property that is, by extension, thought to give the herb its power over lightning.
- Elder (which is believed to keep away evil spirits and witches, improve fertility among stock, and generally

possess magical properties) is also commonly thought to protect against lightning. Feelings about the elder can be very mixed, and in parts of Britain and Ireland, at least, it is considered dangerous to build close to an elder tree, probably because of those same associations with pagan beliefs, witchcraft, and folk tales about tree spirits.

The herbs sage, parsley, and rosemary grow best where the wife is the dominant partner.

Other plants that are traditionally thought to protect against thunder and lightning include:

- holly, which is also good against witches and nightmares
- mistletoe, especially if hung at Christmas
- hawthorn gathered on Ascension Day, always by someone else and not from your own land
- hazel gathered on Palm Sunday (people would take crosses made of hazel twigs to be blessed by their priest).

Dangling Kingfisher

As early as the sixteenth century in the United Kingdom, a stuffed kingfisher was hung in the house to protect the house

All Things Shiny

In parts of the United Kingdom it is believed that, when a storm is imminent, all reflective surfaces in the house need to be covered. This may have begun with a modicum of logic because metal objects do attract lightning. The superstition may simply have extended to a concern with all shiny things. Mirrors, cutlery, and even jugs or pitchers of water are dutifully covered by the superstitious during a storm. Another tradition is to put metal items, such as fire tongs, into the fire during a storm.

from lightning. It was common to see an unfortunate specimen suspended by a piece of string from a beam. A dangling kingfisher also acted as a wind vane, pointing its beak into the wind. This may have been the origin of the superstition and it probably worked outdoors, but it couldn't have been much use inside! Carrying a kingfisher feather in your pocket was also said to bring good luck.

Witch Watch

If you want to fend off witches and the trouble they can bring, there are a number of measures you can take. For example, a variety of plants grown in the garden or hung in the house are said to keep away witches. They are used in different ways, including:

- fennel stuffed in the keyhole or hung over a door

- rosemary planted by the doorstep

- rowan twigs or branches hung above doors, beds, and cupboards

- holly and ivy growing on any part of the house.

In the home, wax from consecrated candles, such as those used at Candlemas or other religious ceremonies, may also protect against witches, if sprinkled around the home. There is evidence of this practice from as early as the sixteenth century in Europe.

Witches were often thought to steal horses and sometimes cows. They were said to ride them to exhaustion during the night. But a stone with a naturally made hole that was hung in the stable was believed to keep witches out. Indoors, similar stones hung over the bed were thought to prevent sleepers from having nightmares. It was said that iron, particularly iron that was cold to the touch, repelled witches, so an iron horseshoe hung over the threshold kept them away from the house, too. A knife, also a cold metal, stuck into a door lintel (or mast, if on a ship or boat), is good luck, and also keeps witches away.

Let Thunder Through

If your chosen method of home storm protection lets you down, there is another superstition you can try: Opening the doors and windows of a house during a storm is said to provide thunder and lightning easy passage through the house, so it will do less damage.

> Never interrupt the making of a bed, or you will be restless during the night.

Baking Bread

Bread baked on Good Friday is thought by some to protect against fire. In some coastal areas of the United Kingdom, where life and livelihood was very much connected to the sea, baking bread is believed to protect against shipwreck if a member of the family is at sea. The baked bread is traditionally hung in the kitchen, which keeps it dry and prevents it from going bad—to bring good luck in baking throughout the year. Bread baked on Good Friday can also be used as a cure for many diseases. In the unlikely event of a fire breaking out, despite the presence of Good Friday bread, an egg laid on Good Friday that is thrown into the heart of the blaze would surely douse the flames.

Warding Off Vermin

In Devon, England, at the turn of the twentieth century, some people believed in following a complicated means of keeping vermin out of the house: "When you hear the first cuckoo in spring, take some of the earth from the place on which your right foot is standing, and sprinkle it on the threshold of your front door; but speak of it to no one. Neither fleas, beetles, earwigs, or vermin of any sort will cross it."

> In Ireland, hearing a dog howling at night when someone in the house is sick is a bad omen.

Shut That Door!

Doors have a long history of superstitions, and many people are still superstitious about shutting all the internal doors in the house before leaving it, as well as shutting the back door before the front, to prevent ill luck. In some areas, swinging on a door is still avoided, in case the swinging blows up a storm at sea. There is a general belief that you should always leave a house through the door you used to enter it, or bad luck will inevitably follow. This is particularly important the first time you enter a house, even if it is not your own. In earlier centuries, most people used the back door more often than the front door because the front of the house was often reserved for guests, and therefore always kept neat and clean. The front door was used for important events, such as bringing home a new baby for the first time or a carrying out a dead person on the journey to their final rest.

If you make your bed on a Friday, you will have bad dreams.

Hanging Horseshoes

Horseshoes are typically hung above a doorway for luck or in a bedroom to keep away nightmares. Most people in Europe and North America hang them with the gap facing downward. Many people in the United Kingdom hang them the other way up to keep the luck from falling through the opening. Gypsies hang horseshoes with the points up, but grooms and blacksmiths hang them points down, like a roof, to ward off bad luck.

Open the Window

Until very recently in the United Kingdom, if someone were thought to be approaching death, others in the house would open all the doors and windows. This was said to allow the spirit of the person to speed on its journey, and not be delayed on its journey to heaven by evil spirits. A similar belief persists today in some hospitals in the West. Nurses open a window when someone has died to allow their soul to leave. Traditionally, sometimes boxes, drawers, and other locks were undone, too, probably so that everything possible was open. When a body was taken from the house for a funeral, many people left the door ajar until the return of the mourners. (Someone else was asked to remain in the house in case of intruders.) If they failed to do this, it was thought that there would soon be another death in the house.

Never sharpen a knife after sunset, or an enemy or thief will enter the house.

The Emperor's Awake

In China, some people often paint the character "fú" (meaning "luck") on their doors for general good luck. They also paint images of "door gods," based on two guards who stayed awake for seven nights to guard their emperor Tai Ling from noisy demons who had disturbed his sleep. After seven nights, the emperor decided he could no longer ask them to stay awake. He had their images painted on his bedroom door instead; these worked just as well in keeping demons away.

When the Cock Crows

In nineteenth-century Britain, many people believed that a cock crowing at a farmhouse door meant a stranger or unexpected visitor would soon arrive. Alternatively, it was sometimes said that the crowing foretold the arrival of some news. A cock crowing at night meant the news would be bad. Even in the nineteenth and twentieth centuries, a crowing cock was still used as a symbol representing a messenger. Other signs that predicted a visitor included:

- accidentally leaving the lid off a teapot while making tea
- finding a tea leaf or stalk floating in your cup of tea
- sweeping out of the door after dark

Be Wary of What You Carry

Many omens predicting future events for a home or its occupants involved people coming into the house, and this could be influenced by what they had with them. For example:

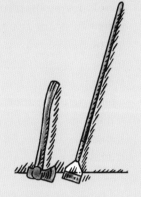

- Walking into a house with the left foot first is thought to bring evil on the occupants, although if you spot the error, you can undo it by walking out again and entering with the right foot.

- Carrying a hoe into a house is bad luck; if you do, walking out backward with it averts the bad luck.

- Never take eggs into a house after sunset or they will not hatch, and they could bring misfortune to the owners of the house.

- Bringing an axe into a house foretells death and, unfortunately, there does not seem to be an antidote to most superstitions involving dying.

- finding soot hanging from the fire grate
- a cat washing its face and paws in the parlor; if the cat washes itself on the doorstep, a member of the clergy will call
- dropping cutlery, and, depending on the item dropped, one could be very specific about the kind of person to be expected, although the symbolism is not universal. One English-language rhyme goes:

"Knife falls, gentleman calls,
Fork falls, lady calls,
Spoon falls, baby calls."

Tools of the Trade

"If a pair of scissors, a knife, or a needle falls to the floor and sticks upright, you will have a visitor before long" is a belief especially popular with dressmakers, milliners, and other people for whom these are tools of the trade. Dropping a pairs of scissors means your lover is unfaithful. If the scissors fall on both points, it indicates a wedding; if they fall on one point, it signifies death. A spoon falling hollow side up may mean a surprise; hollow side down means disappointment. In almost all cases, someone else must pick up the dropped item, not the person who dropped it. And as with knives, if you give someone a pair of scissors as a gift, they should give you a coin in return to avoid cutting the friendship.

In Japan, if a beggar comes to your house, you must throw salt on the doorstep after he leaves to avoid bad luck and misfortune.

Precautions Indoors

Once you are indoors, there are some actions to be avoided, too. For example, it is unlucky to shake hands across a table. Putting certain items on a table, such as shoes or an umbrella, brings general hardship. Dropping your umbrella on the floor, however, prophesies that there will be a murder in the house. Opening it will also bring bad luck, and holding an open umbrella over your head indoors means that there will be a death in the house before the year is out. Use of umbrellas became widespread only in the early nineteenth century, so superstitions relating to them are relatively recent inventions.

Mirrors and Clocks

In many cultures, mirrors and clocks are still believed to be powerful omens. For example, a bride should not see herself in a mirror in her full outfit before the ceremony. And a broken mirror is considered to bring seven years' bad luck, although this is sometimes said to be avoidable if you don't look directly into the broken pieces, then dispose of them in running water. To break a mirror was once an expensive loss, so the superstition may have stemmed from this regrettable situation. Both mirrors and clocks are often covered as a mark of respect when there is a death in the house, probably as a sign that the person has no more worldly needs and time is irrelevant for him or her. A clock falling or stopping is often said to herald the death of a member of the family at the same moment.

Clocks chiming the wrong number of chimes may hold the same meaning, and this has often been said to happen when an important or famous person dies. This reportedly happened when Marie Antoinette was executed.

It is bad luck to go back in a home if you have forgotten something. If you return inside, be sure to look in a mirror and smile.

Passing on the Stairs

If a house has more than one floor, be very careful on the stairs. Passing someone else will bring you both bad luck, or possibly cause you to quarrel or stop being friends. Greeting and touching each other is sometimes said to avert disaster. This superstition may be based on a sense of courtesy because it is sometimes difficult or awkward to pass on a stairway, especially if it is a narrow one. Stumbling down a set of stairs also brings bad luck—perhaps for obvious reasons—but stumbling up them, at least for a woman, means she will soon marry. If she wishes this to come true, she must take care not to look behind her as she continues up the stairs.

Before Birth

To bring a new cradle or stroller into your home before your first baby was born was tempting fate, and so it was avoided. But any babies born afterward would usually reuse the same one, so the superstition didn't apply to them.

In China and other parts of Asia, stone lion and dragon statues are placed by the front door to bring happiness and ward off evil.

Hearths

In the days when people generally heated their homes with a fire in a fireplace, unless you knew someone well and asked first, it was not considered a good idea to stir another person's fire. Seven years was usually the minimum length of time to wait before it was proper to ask. The time period of seven

Salt

Many superstitions are difficult to pin down because we do not have any historical background or basic information about what led to the belief in the first place. In the case of salt, however, there is more information, as it has always been an important and at one time expensive commodity. It is generally agreed that it is unlucky to borrow salt. It may be begged, but the borrower must never return it.

Salt sprinkled on a doorstep after an unwelcome visitor has left ensures that they will never come again; an alternative is to sprinkle salt where they have been, sweep it up, and burn it. In North America, carefully sweeping up spilled salt and throwing it into a fire is said to dry up any future tears. In a few reports, after something causing an ill omen has occurred—for example, putting a lantern on a table—throwing salt on the fire can undo its effects. Salt burning does not appear in historical records before the 1830s, but the belief that salt protects against witchcraft is demonstrably older. A widespread habit to bring good luck when moving into a new house is to have a child sprinkle salt in every hearth and in every corner. Salt sprinkled on the front doorstep is also said to keep evil away. Taking a bar of salt into a new house before moving in any furniture was thought lucky. Helping someone to salt food at the table reputedly brings bad luck to them, hence the saying, "Help me to salt, help me to sorrow." Even today spilled salt causes distress for some people in North America. The superstitious toss salt over their left shoulder to prevent bad luck.

years prehaps relates to idea that this is the length of time it takes for the human body to become a "new person"—and presumably free of lurking evil. In parts of the United Kingdom, it was considered good luck for a stranger to stir the house fire. Bear in mind that, if you visit a friend who is poking the fire as you enter, you're definitely not welcome.

Planting a Chinese jade or money tree (*Crassula ovata*) at your front door is meant to bring wealth and prosperity.

Fireplace Fortune

Traditions revolving around fires and chimneys have been gradually dying out since the introduction of central heating in place of real fires, but there are many superstitions centered on the fireplace.

For example, if soot is clinging to the bar of a grate, it signifies a stranger is expected. If it hangs down from the bar, you can tell which day they will arrive by clapping your hands close to it while listing the days of the week. When the soot falls off, the day is determined. This is called the "stranger on the bar." The size of the hanging piece of soot is significant, too. A small amount of soot represents a child; medium will bring a woman; a large amount, a man.

Two Together Make Trouble

A number of superstitions warn against two people doing certain household chores together. For example, two people making up a fire is thought unlucky because they will quarrel. The most common belief is that it is unlucky for two people to wash their hands together in the same water—although you can make a cross in the water with your finger if you're the second person, or spit in it to undo it the bad luck (which seems to defeat the purpose). Hand washing seems to be the earliest of these superstitions, dating to before the nineteenth century, so it may have been the origin for the others.

In Greece, it is commonly believed that planting a cactus, with its thorny spikes, near the front door will ward off the evil eye.

Fateful Fur and Feathers

Flying Creatures

According to superstition, a bird or bat flying into a house means there will be a death in the family. A bird tapping at the window, or flying or hovering constantly around the house, is commonly held to be a death omen, especially if it is a raven, magpie, or crow—or, less predictably, a robin. An owl on the roof means death, too. If you are a sailor, seagulls squawking around your house foretell your death. If a blackbird nests in your house, however, you will have a year of good luck.

While most large black birds, such as crows and ravens, are symbols of bad luck, rooks have a more mixed reputation. If rooks are building a nest near a house, it is believed to be a sign of prosperity. This is partly because they are supposed to keep crows (which take chickens) away. If the head of the family on whose property hosted the rooks died, they would leave. Or, if the rooks vacated their nests, there would soon be a death in the family. There is a long-held superstition that if the rooks should ever leave the Tower of London, the Britsh and the entire kingdom would fall. Others believe rooks are always harbingers of bad luck.

Crows or rooks were also often thought to carry a plague or fatal disease. A rook or raven perching on a sick person's house foretold their death. They were also predictors of famine and weather—depending on whether they built their nests high or low in the branches of trees; low to the ground signified rain.

27

Other birds had an impact on luck in the home. A single peacock feather indoors is seen as unlucky, and jay feathers in a house mean that you will have no peace from noise. Pigeons alighting on the roof of a house bring death, unless it is a newly married couple's house—in which case they may bring happiness and a family. Swallows and housemartins near the house bring good luck, especially if they build their nests around a house or barn. The superstitious think it bodes ill when the birds leave. There is a traditional folk rhyme:

The robin and the wren
are God Almighty's cock and hen.
The martin and the swallow
are God Almighty's bow and arrow.

The rhyme above exists in various forms, but the meaning is always that these four birds are generally good omens. A magpie perching on a roof means that the house is in no danger of falling. If a magpie chatters 12 times near a house, expect a letter. If it chatters on a tree near the house, a stranger will visit that night. A magpie hopping near a house means good news, usually from afar. And finally, a swan's feather sewn into the pillow will keep a husband faithful.

You should always get out of bed on the right-hand side; getting out on the left is an invitation to the devil.

Moles and Frogs

If a mole burrows under a washhouse or dairy, the mistress of the house will die within the year; if a molehill is found among cabbages, the same fate will happen to the master. Toads in a house were thought to bring bad luck, and they were unceremoniously thrown on the fire in an attempt to avert it. Frogs were good luck, so killing one was unlucky.

Spiders, Rats, and Mice

Spiders in a house have been considered lucky since the eighteenth century. It has been believed that you should never kill a spider, because it is unlucky and may bring poverty. The reason is rarely given, but when it is, it is often that a spider helped Jesus in some way, for example, by spinning a protective web when he was in the cradle to protect him from cold and frost, and to obscure him from the view of King Herod's soldiers. Another version says that Mary and Jesus took refuge in a cave, and a spider quickly wove a web across the entrance to make the pursuers think that no one had recently entered. This story is also told about various heroes and religious figures throughout Europe, Asia, and Africa.

A white moth or a snake is an omen of death, as is a sudden influx of rats or mice. On the other hand, rats or mice leaving a house are also said to mean the death of an occupant. This is connected to—and is possibly an earlier version of—the common phrase about rats leaving a sinking ship.

If you can't get out of bed on the right-hand side, put your right sock and right shoe on before your left to negate possible bad luck.

Fortune and Felines

There is a range of superstitions involving cats, some of which are fortunate and some of which are not.

- In the early sixteenth century, a visitor to an English home would kiss the family cat for luck. White cats, however, were considered to bring bad luck in general.
- Under Scottish superstition, a strange black cat appearing on your doorstep brings wealth.
- A cat sneezing once in the house means rain. A cat sneezing three times means that the family will catch a cold. In Italy, however, it is considered a good omen to

overhear a cat sneezing. In Italy, too, fishermen's wives kept a black cat at home to prevent disaster at sea.

- In sixteenth-century Italy, people thought that, if a cat lay on the bed of a sick person, the person would succumb to the illness. Italians also believed that a cat would not remain in the house with someone about to die, so the cat refusing to stay indoors was a bad omen.
- In England, people say that, if cats desert a house, illness will remain there. In Scotland, there is a belief that, if a cat enters a room with a dead body laid out for burial, the next person to touch it will go blind.
- A black cat entering your house or greeting you at the door of someone else's house is lucky. Early Americans said that a cat sitting with its back to the fire predicted cold weather.

You should never leave a rocking chair rocking when empty, as it is thought to tempt evil spirits to enter your house.

Bees, Crickets, and Blowflies

A bee flying into the house brings good luck. This applies as long as the bee doesn't die indoors, in which case your luck will turn bad. Crickets were generally, though not always, thought lucky, especially on the kitchen hearth. Crickets coming and singing on the hearth of a house meant that riches were coming to the family. In Ireland, their singing was said to keep away fairies that wanted to have the hearth all to themselves at night. Superstitious householders always left a cup of milk for the fairies to drink at night; if the fairies were prevented from arriving by the presence crickets, setting out the milk was unnecessary.

Bluebottles, a type of blowfly that breeds on dead and decaying animal matter, were said to bring fever or death to a person on whom they landed. If a bluebottle could not be chased out of a room, it was believed that the occupant would succumb to fever or die within the year.

To banish evil spirits, walk around your house three times backward and counterclockwise before sunset on Halloween.

Beware of the Bouquet

Certain flowers and plants should not to be brought into the house if its occupants want to avoid bad luck. For example, many people believe that holly can never enter the house except at Christmas, although it is generally considered a lucky plant. Hawthorn, or "may blossom," in the house brought bad luck or death, particularly if it was during the month of May. Many people thought that it smelled like death or the plague, and the superstition may have formed from the association. Yellow flowers, such as primroses and daffodils, were traditionally considered to be bad for chicks or goslings; their presence in a house may prevent them from hatching. This appears to be an example of sympathetic magic because the flowers were sometimes called vegetable goslings, and would obviously "compete" with the animal version.

White flowers such as lilies are still considered unlucky in many households because they are commonly used at funerals, and are therefore associated with death. Red and white flowers mixed are also an omen of death; the color represents blood and bandages, although this may be a modern interpretation.

It is bad luck to bring home flowers from a cemetery or graveyard, for obvious reasons of association. In addition, many people will not have ivy in the house, even at Christmas, when it is one of the traditional decorations. This is probably from its association with old buildings, such as churches and graveyards.

Sickness & Health

In the past, the causes of physical and mental illnesses remained pretty much a mystery—and a frightening one to most people. Folk remedies prevailed and superstitions abounded, born of fear and ignorance. In the beginning, too, doctors were considered little more than quacks. As knowledge in medicine grew, doctors became first the preserve of the wealthy, but traditional remedies were still very much in vogue. Drugs and the medical knowledge to treat many diseases successfully are relatively recent historical developments. It is therefore not surprising that many superstitions grew up around the prevention, treatment, and cure of ailments. Besides cures, there are also many omens for predicting sickness or death.

Malady Matters

In earlier centuries, when there was little knowledge about disease and infection, people could often only guess at how sicknesses originated. Their methods for dealing with them ranged from the benign to the downright gruesome—sometimes more gruesome than the illness itself and definitely not for the faint-hearted or anyone with a weak stomach.

It was sometimes thought that an animal entering the body could cause illness. Some people even claimed, when opening up dead bodies, to have found insects breeding inside them, or frogs, newts, and snakes living there. In order to avoid such an invasion of the body, people were warned not to drink pond water or eat overripe fruit. There are also many stories about witches and demons entering the body and causing sickness or misfortune, but it is impossible to tell if the animal or the witch idea came first.

In the Philippines, it is believed that if you leave the house before the dishes are washed, someone in the family will die.

Birds on the Brain

Birds are often thought to be the cause of sickness. In Germany, for example, it is said that you must burn any hairs you comb out of your head. Otherwise, if a bird carries them to its nest, you will suffer from headaches. If a starling takes your hair for its nest, you will develop cataracts and go blind. In France, it is said that a child who touches a wren's nest will develop pimples. In Morocco, however, if that happens, rubbing the inside of a freshly slaughtered sheep's skin on the face is believed to remedy the problem—if you can stand it.

33

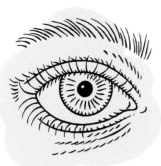

The Evil Eye

A common superstition in most of Europe and in some Middle Eastern cultures was the fear of someone with an evil eye. Some people thought that, as opposed to entering the body, someone had only to stare at him or her with their evil eye—known as "overlooking"—to cause sickness. Witches supposedly obtained their evil eye through a pact with the devil. Other people could simply inherit it, or be born with it as an accident of fate. For example, anyone who looked

Warts and All

There is an abundance of superstitious cures for warts. Many give at least the appearance of working because warts often go away without any treatment. In the days before we knew about viruses, warts must have seemed mysterious. Juice from the plant celandine is one of the most popular cures. This superstition has some grounding in science because the plant contains alkaloids, including chelidonin and chelerythrin, which may help to treat skin ailments.

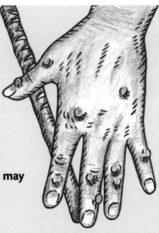

Common beliefs to avoid getting warts:

- Do not wash your hands in water that has been used to boil eggs.

- The old standard: Never touch a toad, particularly if you are a child.

- Avoid any physical contact with a wart or blood from a wart.

Common beliefs to cure warts:

- Rub a piece of bread or raw meat on the wart, and bury the contaminated bread or meat. As the food decays, so will the wart, until it eventually disappears.

- Count the warts and make the same number of notches on a stick. Bury the stick or throw it away. The person who finds the stick will inherit the warts.

- Sell your warts to someone for a pin or coin. For example, witches could buy warts for pins. Your warts will disappear, but the buyer will not necessarily develop them.

Red or Dead

Over much of Europe and across several cultures, including the ancient Romans, much of northern Europe and Romany and Jewish tradition, red ribbon, thread, or wool were often used to protect against supernatural beings, witches, or demons. Tying something red around a baby's cradle prevented fairies from stealing the child. If a child had already been sick, putting a red ribbon on it would stop the sickness from returning. Red thread tied around cows' tails before turning them into the field for the first time in spring protected them from the evil eye and elf-shot—being injured by a bolt or arrow shot by an elf, which could affect both people and animals.

Tying a red thread around your neighbor's gate would transfer your disease to him or her. In Britain, lunacy was thought to be curable if you tied a plant called clove-wort with a red thread around your neck, but it had to be done during a waning moon in April or early October. In Jewish tradition, the thread used in building the first temple was red, and it is a reminder that one should be as humble as the worm from which the thread came. This type of humility was considered the best protection from the evil eye.

different or stood out from the majority of the community, or those who were born on a particular day, were often said to have the evil eye. There are even stories of people who believed that they had the evil eye, and were careful to avoid looking directly at others to avoid harming them or being accused of hurting them.

Luckily, in the Middle East, amulets with an eye painted on to them—still seen commonly today—were available to ward off the evil eye. In northern Europe, holed stones, horseshoes, and red thread were all similarly recommended.

In Greece, a blue charm with an eye painted in the center of it, worn on a necklace or bracelet, protects against the evil eye.

Rhyming for Health

Meeting an ambulance was traditionally thought to be bad for your health. This belief may have been logical and grounded in historical fact; when open carts were used to transport the sick or dead, infection was possible and probably rife. This particular superstition hung on as late as the twentieth century, when the superstitious still had rituals and rhymes to ward off the bad luck of seeing an ambulance.

In Britain, you would hold your collar until you saw a four-legged animal, preferably a black dog. Until the animal appears, chant the rhyme: *"Touch collar, never swallow, touch your nose, touch your toes, never go in one of those."*

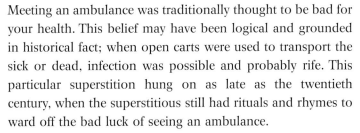

If you want extra insurance, spit, cross your fingers, or touch wood. Lots of people still do this when they don't want something they say to become a premonition.

Positive Prevention against Illness

Traditionally, there were positive actions you could take to prevent a variety of illnesses. Keeping a spider in a walnut shell, for example, was thought by many to prevent plague or fever. To prevent epilepsy and seizures in general, it was believed that you should wrap a dried frog in silk and wear it around your neck. In Kenya, the superstitious wear a black bracelet as protection against disease in general.

Beware!

If you are walking anywhere in Morocco, and someone is sitting in your path, do not step over him or her. Be sure to walk around them. If you step over the person, rather than taking evasive action, his or her growth will be stunted.

Sleep Right, Sleep Tight!

A bed, with its obvious links to sickness, childbirth, and death, was intrinsic to many superstitions about health.

For example, the superstitious consider the orientation of the bed to be important for health and restful sleep. Unfortunately, there is little agreement as to the best orientation: Some say north–south is best; others say east–west. Some assert that the bed is best aligned with the floorboards; others believe it is the beams in the ceiling that are your guide to being healthy and happy. The correct alignment will also help prevent a long, drawn-out death.

Making the bed has an effect on health, too. It is often said to be unlucky to turn a mattress on a Friday or a Sunday. If you are ill in bed, turning the mattress will prevent recovery.

> "Ah they put pigeons' feathers in the pillows—no wonder I couldn't die!"
>
> —*Wuthering Heights*, Emily Brontë

The superstitious believe that an onion cut in half and placed under a bed will draw off fever and poisons. And keep your hat off the bed—otherwise bad luck will follow.

Alternative Antidotes

Superstitious Cures

No matter how many measures people took to avoid illness, they still got sick. Luckily, there were cures based on superstitions as well. Most of them didn't work, for a variety of reasons, but they did give people hope. And, of course, on the occasions when sick people recovered, it was all attributed to the charm, folk remedy, or ritual used during the illness.

Some superstitious cures included:

- taking a hair from a head, making a sandwich of it between two slices of buttered bread, and feeding it to a dog, for example, to cure a cough. Some people said a rhyme to accompany the feeding: "Eat well, you hound; may you be sick and I be sound."
- breaking two loaves that had stuck together in the oven over the head of a tongue-tied person to cure the problem.
- if you lived in Germany, where freckles were considered to be an affliction, using rainwater that had fallen on a tomb to remove them—most people just try lemon juice.

Feline Folk Remedies

Superstitious people sometimes considered cats to be dangerous, especially for babies. It was believed that a cat could steal a baby's breath, and cause its death. A common superstition was that if a cat got into a baby's bed, it would lie on the baby and suffocate it. It is possible that these two beliefs were linked. Cats and their association with magic and the occult—particularly black cats—often feature in superstitions for curing illnesses. Some of the beliefs included:

- Styes could be cured by stroking the affected eye with the end of a cat's tail.

- A small amount of a cat's blood, usually from the ear or tail, would cure erysipelas (an acute skin infection that produced shaking, fever, headaches, and vomiting), ringworm, and shingles.

- A person raving with fever could be calmed and cured by simply casting or passing a cat over him or her.

- In an extremely unpleasant ritual for a relatively minor ailment, a cure for a swollen knee was to kill a cat, split it lengthwise and, while it was still warm, bind it around the affected knee.

- standing at a crossroads and chanting: "Stye, Stye, leave my eye, take the next one coming by," to transfer a stye from one person to another.

In Britain, a necklace of amber beads was said to prevent illness and cure colds.

Herbal Magic

Many folk cures involved plants or nuts because they were easy to get hold of and, provided the plant or nut itself wasn't toxic, most cures were relatively harmless. Some, such as aloe vera, did possess beneficial effects later borne out by science.

- **Acorns** had a number of uses, most of which probably originally stemmed from them being the fruit of the sacred oak tree of Celtic and pagan belief. They were carried or placed under a bed to cure cramps or rheumatism, and eaten to relieve a stomachache, loose bowels, and fever. In Britain, carrying an acorn in your pocket was said to help alleviate the effects of old age.
- **Dandelions**, despite or perhaps because of a reputation for causing bedwetting, were commonly used for making tea to cure illnesses, including kidney and liver problems.
- **Elder** had a variety of uses, even though it had a dubious reputation in many ways because of its links with pagan beliefs and witchcraft. Elder twigs could be inserted into the ear as a cure for an earache. The bark, wood, flowers, and berries were powdered or boiled, or made into teas, ointments, or wine. The resulting medications were used for toothache, colds, coughs, gout, acne, and freckles.

    An elder necklace was worn to cure teething problems, epilepsy, and whooping cough, and it was considered especially effective if it were made from a tree growing in a churchyard. Carrying a piece of elder was said to prevent saddle sores during long-distance journeys.

Breathing In

Whooping cough was common but frightening childhood ailment in times before vaccination was widespread. For the wealthy, a trip to the sea or the mountains, or even to another country, was an option.

For most people, however, any sort of a trip was out of the question. Instead, for children who contracted the often fatal disease, there was another superstition: It was believed that inhaling the pungent fumes created while making gas, burning lime or charcoal, or making and using tar would cure the illness, and so children were intentionally exposed to fumes. Among other remedies to cure whooping cough, the superstitious recommended:

- crossing water three times

- eating roasted mice

- riding a bear

- drinking milk lapped by a ferret

- hanging small live animals or creatures such as spiders, woodlice, and caterpillars in a bag around the sufferer's neck until the animal has died

- swallowing small live frogs or making them into a soup

Pining Away

In a Chinese story, a man named Zhao Qu had been ill for many years. His family left him in the mountains to die. But an immortal gave him some medicine containing pine oil, and Zhao Qu returned home to live to more than 100 years of age. His hair never turned white, and his teeth never fell out. Whatever this story's provenance, in modern-day China, pine oil is still believed to promote long life.

Healing Tree Rituals

Sympathetic magic sometimes played an important role in superstitious cures. A child born with a hernia, for example, might undergo a ritual in which a tree was split and the child passed through it a certain number of times. The actual passing had to be in a certain direction, too, for it to have any effect—although this varied enormously. Once the ritual was complete, the tree was tied up again. It was said that as the tree's rupture healed, so, too, would the child's.

Carrying rattlesnake rattlers in your hat will cure a headache.

Cooling Burns

Traditional folk remedies for burns included applying turpentine, goose droppings, honey, aloe vera, apple cider vinegar, buttermilk, or mashed potatoes to an affected area. In the days when cooking was done over an open fire or a range, these cures were no doubt much in demand.

Magic was also sometimes used; often the victim would stand in front of a fire and let the sparks fall on him or her. In Ireland, it was believed that someone who licked the underside of a lizard became able to withstand hot things, and could thereafter cure burns simply by licking them.

Keep Chilled

Some traditional cures for chilblains—inflamed sores or swellings—are to thrash them with holly, bathe them in urine, or rub them with onions, goose fat, or snow. If a baby's feet are rubbed in the first snowfall after its birth, it is said that it will never suffer from chilblains.

To cure a cold, grate onions and use them as a mustard plaster on your chest. At the very least, the fumes will clear your sinuses.

Earaches

There are many strange earache cures from around the world. Most of them, perhaps reasonably, involve placing an object in the ear. Often the objects are warm, which were thought to help ears blocked with wax because the warmth might soften the wax, and relieve the pressure. The problem came with the items chosen for insertion. These included a small baked onion, hot eel oil, whiskey, hot salt, or a hot currant.

Whenever you pass a cemetery, always hold your breath to avoid inhaling the spirit of someone who has recently died.

A Sore Point

Alabaster was not only used to create statues; in its powdered form, it was also added to an ointment for sore

The Hair of the Dog That Bit Me

Hydrophobia, or rabies, is still a common disease in many countries, and it is more easily spread in some places than in others. Symptoms that arise after being bitten by a rabid animal include excessive salivation and/or aggression, and general weakness. Rabid animals are usually killed.

In terms of superstition, if a healthy dog contracted the disease after it had bitten someone, the bitten person would also contract rabies through a type of sympathetic magic. In this case—if the dog's owner agreed—the animal would be drowned. Sometimes its heart or liver was cut out and given to the victim to eat. Some of the dog's hair would also be eaten by the victim or simply applied to the wound. This is probably the origin of the saying "the hair of the dog that bit me," which is now usually used in reference to having an alcoholic drink in the morning to cure a hangover. The saying was proverbial by the middle of the sixteenth century in England; it appears in Heywood's 1546 Proverbs as "A heare of the dog that bote us last night."

legs and other parts of the body. In the early twentieth century, alabaster was used in Wales as a cure for rabies, when drunk in milk. Alabaster from statues erected in or near churches was thought to be particularly effective, and many statues were defaced because they supplied this "healing" substance.

Wet and Dry

Feeding a child a teaspoon of honey at bedtime or a tea made of hot water and corn silk, winter evergreen, or prince's pine were two relatively benign "cures" for bedwetting in children. There is also an unusual—and more extreme—folk remedy for bedwetting from Sussex, England. It was believed that if a child with bedwetting problems urinated on the open grave of someone of the opposite sex—in the morning while the first part of the service was read—the child's bedwetting would cease. The thought of having to go through that ritual humiliation again may have been the key to this "cure."

Stopping Seizures

Epilepsy, with its alarming episodes of seizures, produced a number of superstitious beliefs. Unfortunate sufferers were thought to be possessed by evil spirits or bewitched. Cures included killing a cockerel in the place where the first seizure occurred or burying a live cockerel under the floorboards in the same spot. The blood of a mole was also believed to help sufferers. Alternatively, a small bag with hair from a donkey's back was believed to cure seizures—and at least more tolerable for the squeamish.

Thunder at the end of a funeral ceremony is considered a good omen, because it means that the person's soul has reached heaven.

Blessed Beast of Burden

In a transference superstition practiced in Ireland and parts of Britain, a child suffering from whooping cough was passed under and over a donkey, usually three times, and often facing a particular direction. An alternative was to ride a male donkey, usually backward. This cure may be related to the Christian belief that the donkey is a blessed animal. There is a fable that the cross of dark hairs that appear on the back of a donkey is a reminder of the donkey that carried Jesus into Jerusalem. In addition, it was a donkey that carried the holy family on their way to the stable in Bethlehem, and their later flight into Egypt to prevent Herod from killing the infant Jesus. Also, children suffering whooping cough were often given donkey's milk, a cure that dates back at least to the ancient Romans and can be found in many places worldwide, including Europe and Africa.

Transference

The principle of transference, where the disease is passed to another object or person, was believed to cure whooping cough and other ailments, including boils and rheumatism. For example, if a sufferer crawled or passed through a bramble that was rooted at both ends to form an arch, they

If the coffee grounds in the bottom of your cup form a straight line, expect a death soon.

would be cured of their illness. This cure was known in Britain as early as the seventeenth century, when it was recommended as a cure for a horse that had been poisoned by a shrew.

Other transference superstitions involved the simple notion of someone "buying" your illness or affliction, such as warts or a common cold. Fortunately, the buyer didn't have to be brave enough to take on your disease, as the magic was in the act of "buying," rather than him or her having to take it over so that you would be healthy.

Forged!

Forge water, the water a blacksmith used for cooling metal, was a common cure for warts, consumption, and sores. This superstition originated in Britain and Ireland, but its influence spread to North America with the early settlers, and thrived in areas such as the Ozarks—as many superstitions did.

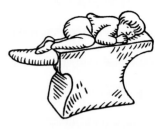

For children with rickets or who were generally not in robust good health, a blacksmith would pass his tools over the sufferers or give the pretense (one hopes!) of hitting them with his hammer while they were laid on his anvil.

Stopping the Flow

Spiderwebs provided a natural and traditional remedy for a bleeding wound, as mentioned by Bottom, a character in Shakespeare's late-sixteenth-century play *A Midsummer Night's Dream*: "I shall desire you of more acquaintance, good Master Cobweb; if I cut my finger I shall make bold with you." Other treatments used for a wound included applying puffballs, plantain, or primrose leaves to it, although the spiderwebs were the most common remedy.

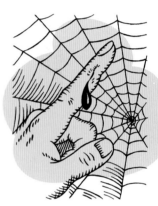

Charms and so-called charmers were also used, to little effect, as this article from London's *Daily Telegraph* of July

Powdered Toad

A record written in 1900 in Devon, England, recommended the following remedy for stopping bleeding using a toad:

> Take a fine full-grown toad, kill him, then take three bricks and keep in a very hot oven until they are red hot. Take one out and place the toad upon it; when the brick is cold remove the toad; then take the other bricks and place the toad on them successively until he be reduced to powder.
>
> Then take the toad-ashes and sew them up carefully in a silk bag one-and-a-half inches square. When one is bleeding place this bag on the heart of the sufferer, and it will instantly stay the bleeding of the nose or any wound.

1887 reports: "A farm labourer named Thos. Ryder, residing at Cornwood, a village in Devonshire, was sharpening his scythe on Tuesday, when he cut his wrist, and severed two of the arteries. His friends, instead of securing medical assistance, sent for a man and his wife who have a local reputation as 'charmers,' and these people endeavoured to stop the flow of blood by the ceremony of 'charming,' Ryder, seeing how fruitless these efforts were, begged to be taken to the hospital at Plymouth, some eight miles off...Ryder died of loss of blood before he got there."

It's best not to bury any female relatives in black; otherwise, they will come back to haunt the family.

Rheumatism

Superstitions for rheumatism were numerous and varied. Many of them included carrying an object, usually in the pocket. Helpful objects were sulfur, brimstone, nutmeg, acorns, hazelnuts, horse chestnuts, or a small potato. You could also try a hare's or mole's foot, or the jaw of a female hedgehog. Other cures included applying substances to the affected area; stinging nettles and bee stings were said to be effective and, in fact, modern science shows some evidence that the latter may have some realistic basis. Cowpats, badger fat, herring skins, and paraffin were also

Put a Cork in It

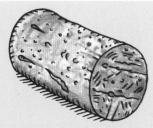

In a remedy that has become widespread worldwide, cork is sometimes suggested as a cure for leg cramps, although where to put it is a matter of individual taste. You could put it under your pillow or mattress, between your toes, around your wrist, or just anywhere under the covers.

Bless You!

**The origin and purpose of saying "Bless you!" or "God bless!"
after someone sneezes is not known.**

In medieval England, a sneeze was believed to be the soul
trying to escape the body, and saying "Bless you" forced it
back in again. It was also thought that sneezing opened the body up
to potential invasion by evil spirits, or even the devil himself! During
the Black Plague, or Black Death, which swept across Central Asia, Europe,
and the Middle East in the fourteenth century, people supposedly said
"God bless you" after someone sneezed, both to cure the sneezer and to
protect the person saying the blessing from catching the infection. However, sneezing was not
one of the symptoms of the plague, or Black Death, so this seems an unlikely habit!

Today Muslims say the equivalent of "Thank God" after a sneeze, and people in many
countries say "Good health," such as in Germany, where this expression is "Gesundheit!" The
earliest English reference to people consciously "saluting," or acknowledging, a sneeze out of
superstition is in Caxton's 1483 *Golden Legend*, which tells of a great pestilence among the
early Christians, causing sudden death, often with a sneeze. In this case, saying "God bless
you" was a wish for the dead person's soul to go to heaven. Some Victorian writers noted that
the "ancients" believed that a person sneezed only once, then died, and attributed the
custom to them. In fact, there is a reference to a similar ritual by Pliny the Elder, who asked in
Natural History, "Why do we say 'Good health' to those who sneeze?"

In some parts of the world, such as Greece, sneezing once means that someone is talking
about you. In China and Japan, the superstition is further embellished: one sneeze—
someone is saying something good about you; two sneezes in a row—someone is saying
something bad; multiple sneezes in a row—expect a cold (who said superstitions couldn't
be practical?). Or you could hope to sneeze three times in a row, which many people
consider a sign of good luck.

recommended. Javanese people rub pepper into their
fingernails and toenails.

For cramps as well as rheumatism, some superstitions
recommended wearing an eelskin garter or a red cloth tied

around your body. The natural warmth of animals was also sometimes used; the skin of a newly flayed sheep, for example, was placed on the limbs of the sufferer in an attempt to alleviate the pain. But, according to one superstition, it seems you would never suffer from rheumatism if you always put on stockings left leg first—far easier all round on the joints and on the stomach.

If a nurse knocks over a chair, a new patient will be arriving soon.

Another common way to ward off rheumatism or leg cramps was to carry a "cramp-bone"—the patella or knuckle bone of a sheep—with you at all times. Simple, really. Yet another superstition recommended that you place your shoes

Dead Man's Hand

In Europe, it was once commonly believed that a dead man's hand, particularly that of a man who had been hanged for murder or another crime, had healing powers. Lady Charlotte Wake of Scotland in 1909 recalled the story of how she was cured of a strawberry birthmark by the laying on of a dead man's hand, and how a widow frequently examined her cheek, "as the marks, as she told my nurse, would certainly fade away as he turned into dust…"

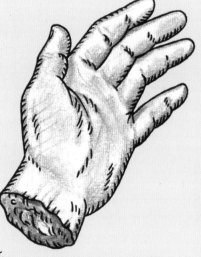

A stroke of a dead man's hand was also said to cure an enlargement of the thyroid gland, scrofula, lumps and other swellings, or skin complaints. However, this type of touch could also bring disaster. If the man had died of typhoid, for example, touching the hand could infect the sufferer.

Incidentally, if there was an execution by hanging, this was good news for someone with a toothache. According to superstition, rubbing a piece of wood from a gallows cured an aching tooth or gum.

Powerful Placebo

Even today, Tibetans can be very superstitious, and many old beliefs, particularly those relating to omens and illness, persist among some people. In Tibet, if a doctor has run out of the medicine someone needs, he writes its name on paper and the person swallows the paper instead. It is believed to have the same effect as the actual medicine.

in a T- or cross-shape on the floor or bed, or leave your shoes upside down at night. The power of the cross would work during the day, too. If you had a cramp, it was suggested that you lick your forefinger and draw a cross on the top of the foot or shoe as a quick fix.

If a married woman walks on a grave, she or her child will have clubfoot.

A Weighty Solution

Naturally formed hollow stones—with a loose part inside that rattled—were called "aetites" or "eagle stones" because it was believed that they were found in eagles' nests. They were often used in childbirth, as a painkiller, tied to a woman's arm. When the birth was imminent, the stone would be transferred to a leg, where it was believed to help ease and quicken the birth process. These stones were often kept in bags that had strings attached so they could be tied onto the woman. They were usually loaned to anyone who needed them.

Omens of Death

Death is an inevitable part of the human condition, and its eventual occurrence is the one thing we can predict with certainty. However, people have always sought ways to predict it in more specific detail. The superstitious watch for omens,

When Death Comes Knocking

Many superstitious sounds herald impending death:

- If a church door rattles unusually, it is said that by the end of the week a corpse will be passing through it.

- If you hear the first cuckoo of the year when you are in bed, you or another member of your family will soon be ill or die.

- Unexplained knocking at the door, window, sick person's bed, or anywhere else in the house foretells death. Three measured knocks are less easily explained than a single knock, so they are often thought to be more portentous. And if the sound is repeated three times in the night, or on three successive nights, it is even more ominous.

- If a clock strikes in a church while hymns are sung, or during another particular part of the ceremony, it is often said to mean a death in the parish will soon follow. Some superstitious people turn off the church clock's striking mechanism during services.

The sounds said to predict death can be roughly divided into three categories:

- Random sudden, unexpected, unexplainable noises around the house, such as crashes and bangs

- Naturalistic sounds connected with actions that will take place after death, but heard before the actual death. These include, for example, the sounds of a coffin being made or placed on chairs, funeral carts—especially if they seem to stop outside your door—footsteps or the voices of people gathering, and any knocking on the door or windows.

- Known and expected environmental sounds, such as a dog howling or water dripping. The sound of the deathwatch beetle falls into this category because even people who know what causes the sound—maggots of the beetle inside wood—may hear it very clearly on a quiet night when someone is ill, and link it subconsciously to death. This particular beetle makes a sound like a ticking watch, and may also be linked to the passing of time. The deathwatch superstition goes back to at least the 1700s.

such as a picture falling off the wall for no apparent reason or a bird pecking at the window, which might foretell a coming death. In many cultures, overhearing the hoot of an owl could also presage death—although in Malaysia and on a far happier note, if a pregnant woman hears an owl, it means that her baby will be a girl.

If three people are photographed together, the one in the middle will die first. Never has position been so important.

Snuffed Out

A once-popular superstition was the way a "winding-sheet," or piece of melting wax that wound around a candle when the flame guttered, was seen to predict the death of the person sitting across from it. Since electric lighting has replaced candles, the superstition is obviously becoming less known. Perhaps the surge in aromatherapy will rekindle interest. It is believed, however, that if the wind blows out a candle on an altar, or the church lights grow dim, the clergyman or minister will soon die. Dreaming of a black candle is another omen of death or illness—not restricted to people of the cloth—and, if a candle flame turns blue, someone is about to die.

Brown Bread, You're Dead

Bread, known as the staff of life, is also often associated with death. Taking three loaves of bread from the oven at once, dropping a loaf while taking it out of the oven, or a loaf that split across the top while the dough was being shaped all foretold an imminent death. And a loaf with a hole in it signified a grave or coffin, indicating that someone close to the family would die soon.

Love & Romance

There is, perhaps, little in life as uncertain as love—at least in terms of the kind of love that has you sighing aimlessly, mooning hopelessly over your beloved's picture, and composing sonnets in iambic pentameter on bar napkins. Romantic love is an emotion we can't explain. But, as we are human, we try to make sense of it, control it, and pin it down. For the superstitious, there are countless ways of doing this, including rituals to find out whom we shall love, omens to tell us if we are to meet someone or if our lover is unfaithful, and ways to ensure his or her return.

Heartache, Heartbreak

Much like sickness, love was likely to come to most people sooner or later, so any superstitious ritual carried out or omen observed would appear to be fulfilled, and the superstition thus reinforced.

Leaf of Love

In Britain up until the nineteenth century or so, finding a twig of ash with an even number of leaves was thought lucky, just as finding a four-leaf clover still is today. They could also be used to summon a woman's future husband. She would pick the twig of ash and recite the following couplet:

> *The even-ash leaf in my hand*
> *The first I meet shall be my man.*

Next, she would put it into her glove and recite:

> *The even-ash leaf in my glove*
> *The first I meet shall be my love.*

Finally, she would place the leaf into her bosom and say:

> *The even-ash leaf in my bosom*
> *The first I meet shall be my husband.*

Soon afterward, she could expect her future husband to arrive—and hopefully be happy with the candidate supplied.

A two-leaf, rather than a four-leaf, clover could be used in a simpler way. It was placed in a shoe, and the next person of the opposite sex you met was your spouse-to-be—or at least had the same name as the future spouse. (This type of escape clause probably saved many young people from dismay when they met someone they found undesirable.) An ivy leaf in a pocket was said to have a similar effect.

Apples and Love

Apples are often associated with love; the fruit Eve was said to have given Adam in the Garden of Eden is often described as an apple. One well-known superstition says if someone peels an apple in one piece and throws it over his or her shoulder or head, it will fall in the shape of a future lover's initial. The earliest written reference to this ritual is in John Gay's 1714 pastoral poem *The Shepherd's Week*:

> *This mellow pippin which I pare around*
> *My shepherd's name shall flourish on the ground*
> *I fling the unbroken paring over my head*
> *Upon the grass a perfect L is read.*

In the Channel Islands, girls would try to bring about a dream of their lover by sticking 18 pins into a golden apple—nine in the eye and nine in the stem—tying their left garter around it, and placing it under their pillow at night. Eating an apple in front of a mirror by the light of a candle (sometimes while combing or brushing hair) was supposed to cause the image of your future love to appear in the mirror as if he were looking over your shoulder.

But apple seeds seem to have the most uses in superstitious love rituals. To find out from which direction your lover will arrive, squeeze a seed between your fingers, and observe where it flies out. Alternatively, you can throw a seed in the air and let it fall to the ground or simply shake it between your cupped hands. Your love will come from the direction in which the seed points.

Another superstition includes placing two apple seeds next to each other on a fire shovel and placing them in the fire. The woman names the one for herself, and the other for a particular gentleman in whom she is interested. If, in the heat of the fire, they fly off in different directions, there will be no romantic relationship. If the seeds burn together without flying off, the man will never propose. If they both fly off on the same side of the shovel, however, the pair will marry. If you have a number of potential partners in mind, you can find out which of them loves you best by sticking apple seeds— each named for one of the lovers—onto your face. The last seed to fall off represents the person who loves you wholeheartedly.

If a girl shelling peas found nine in a pod, she could place it above a doorway or on the threshold. The first male to enter after this would be either her sweetheart or husband. Another way to encourage true romance was to cut your nails on a Saturday; you would then see your love on Sunday.

Apparently, salty soup can be taken as a sure sign that the cook is in love.

Midsummer Rose (or Christmas Rose)

In the hope of finding love, a girl could gather a rose on Midsummer Eve (June 21st)—the summer solstice or longest day of the year—then carry the rose home walking backward and in silence. If she kept it carefully wrapped in white paper until the upcoming Christmas Day, and wore it then, her future husband would take it from her.

Look Back in Hope

In another ritual for love divination, popular in the West Country in England and rural areas such as Norfolk, a girl would go into a churchyard on Midsummer Eve (June 21st), the celebration marking the summer solstice, and throw a handful of hemp seed behind her, then run away. If she was brave enough to turn her head and look behind her as she ran, she would see her future husband running after her with a scythe. If she was to die an old maid, she would see a coffin or hear a bell. This ritual was also known to occur on Halloween, Christmas Eve, St. Mark's Eve, and Valentine's Day, and also with other kinds of seed, including barley, linseed, and fern seed. In the novel *The Woodlanders* (1887) by Thomas Hardy, this superstitious ritual is given a little help. In his story, interested boys hide themselves so that they can be seen at the right moment by the right girl, while other villagers observe the proceedings.

In Sweden, where midsummer celebrations rival those at Christmas, young people traditionally pick bouquets of seven or nine different flowers, and put them under their pillow. This is supposed to lead to dreams about their future spouse.

Auspicious Days

Many love-related rituals were performed only on certain days of the year, including St. Mark's Eve (April 24th), Halloween, Christmas Eve, St. Agnes's Eve (January 20th) and of course, Valentine's Day. They were often almost interchangeable, in that often a particular ritual for divining love performed on a particular saint's day in one place was carried out on another saint's day entirely somewhere else. Details may have varied slightly, but the intent was always the same.

Wraith Watching

In parts of England from the seventeenth to the late nineteenth centuries, particularly the north of the country, St. Mark's Eve was a vigil for watching for the ghosts of those who would die in the coming year. In a slightly more positive extension of this superstition, a man who sat in a barn at midnight on St. Mark's Day (April 25th) was supposed to be able to see his future wife walk in one door and out the other.

Walk backward to a pear tree and around it three times on Christmas Eve to see the spirit or image of a future husband.

Girls working in a kitchen would often perform a special ritual on St. Mark's Day, too. Laying the supper table for the evening meal just before midnight, they would sit away from the table. As the clock struck midnight, it was said that the wraith, or spirit, of one of the girls' future husbands would enter and sit on one of the chairs.

Another ritual designed to reveal the wraith of your husband-to-be was sometimes performed on Christmas Eve or Halloween. A girl would wash her shirt or blouse, hang it before the fire to dry, and watch in silence, usually with the door open to ease the path of any spirits. Eventually she would see the wraith enter the room and turn the shirt. Of course, it could also be said that tiredness is a great aid in firing the imagination!

Veiled Truth

In another Halloween superstition, an unmarried woman would place a veil over a mirror. When the veil was removed at midnight, the face of her future husband would appear in the glass—an adult version of trick-or-treat, perhaps?

Cut a fern straight across the stem, and the veins will be in the shape of your future husband's initial.

Dream Lovers

In Ireland, a boy would traditionally gather ten ivy or sometimes yarrow leaves in silence, then throw away the tenth leaf. The nine remaining leaves were left outside until bedtime, when he brought them in and placed them in his right sock and under his pillow, saying the following rhyme:

Nine ivy leaves I place under my head
To dream of the living and not the dead
If ere I be married or wed unto thee
To dream of her tonight, and for her to see
The color of her hair, and the clothes that she wears
And the day she'll be wedded to me.

It was often girls or women who wanted to dream of their future spouses or lovers, however, and there was a huge variety of rituals that were performed in an attempt to make this wish come true.

St. Thomas's Onion

According to English folklore, a love-divination ritual popular from the seventeenth to eighteenth centuries and almost unchanged during that time was carried out on St. Thomas's Eve (December 20). A girl would peel an onion, wrap it in a clean handkerchief, and place it under her pillow. Sometimes she would stick pins in it first, usually nine, and if there was a particular boy she hoped to dream of, she might name a central pin and stick the other eight around it. One variation of the rhyme that went with the ritual is as follows:

Good St. Thomas, do me right
And let my true love come tonight
That I may see him in the face
And him in my kind arms embrace.

If you forget to put the pillows in place when you are making a bed, you will not be married in that year.

Divining with Paper and Ink

Paper and ink are used in a number of superstitious rituals for divining the name of a future lover. Write the names of three men you have an interest in on different pieces of paper, roll each paper into a ball of bread, and throw them into water. The one that rises will contain your future husband's name. Or you could just write the man's initial, which widens the possibilities somewhat. On St. Thomas's Eve (December 20), cut out paper shapes for each the letter of the alphabet, put them in a bowl of water under your bed, and in the morning those that are floating represent the initials of your lover. This superstition can also be performed on Christmas Eve, St. Valentine's Eve, or Midsummer Eve. Or to dream of a certain man, write his name on paper, burn it, and put the ash under your pillow.

A Simple Dumb-Cake

From the seventeenth to the late nineteeth century in England, girls would participate in a "dumb-cake" ritual. The ingredients of the dumb-cake differed from place to place, but the ceremony was more or less the same. The ritual itself, like many British and Irish rituals, seems to have its roots in paganism.

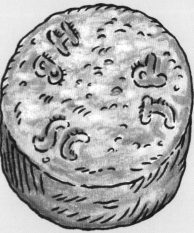

A cooperative effort, the ritual took place late in the evening on St. Mark's Eve, St. Agnes's Eve, or Christmas Eve, or Halloween—all standard dates for love divinations. Typically, three, five, or seven girls took part because odd numbers were regarded as lucky in English tradition.

To begin, each girl stood on something they had never stood on before, such as a baking pan or dishcloth. The girls grouped themselves around the counter, or table, with a large sheet of paper in front of them. One after another, the girls took a handful of flour and placed it on the paper. Each girl then added a pinch of salt and some water, and began to mix the dough, kneading and working it together. In some recipes, soot or even urine was added. Similar to eating a raw herring on St. Agnes's Day), this was presumably to test the girls' resolve. The dough was formed into a thin cake large enough to write the initials of all the girls on it. Together, they lifted it onto a baking sheet and laid it before the fire. They then waited until midnight.

In some versions, the girls ate the cake before retiring to bed to dream of their future husbands. Those who were to remain unmarried were said to dream about an open grave, churchyards, or a ring that didn't fit or crumbled when put on. In other variations, the wraith of the girl to be married first was said to appear and touch her initials on the cake as the clock struck midnight. Central to the entire ritual was that it had to take place in complete silence. If anyone spoke, the efforts of all the girls would be for nothing—not just the girl who spoke out of turn. This is what led to the cake being called "dumb," rather than the name being a reflection of the intelligence of those involved!

In Latin America, it is believed that if someone passes a broom over a single woman's feet, the woman will never marry.

Other objects that could be put under the pillow included: wedding cake—which is still a popular superstition today—a knotted garter, or a piece of a briar that had grown into the ground, forming a loop that you had crept through at night. In one record, girls described digging up plantain plants and looking for a piece of coal beneath their roots, so that they could put the coal under their pillows. Even shoes placed in a T-shape beneath the bed were thought to induce a girl to dream of a future lover.

Candles

Girls sometimes stuck pins into a candle in an attempt to force their sweetheart to pay more attention or to come and visit them. A superstition also held that you could sit in silence, usually on either St. Mark's or St. Agnes's Eve, and watch a small candle (previously stolen) until it burned blue—when you would see your future husband walk across the room. Once a candle had melted, the shape of the wax could tell you whether you were to be lucky in love, for example, if it resembled a ring or heart shape.

If three, or sometimes four, candles were placed close together, especially on the same table, a wedding was imminent. However, for some people, three candles placed together predicted death. Perhaps this left a vacancy for a new bride or groom. Whatever the case, the placement of the candles had to be unconscious, and someone else would have to notice and make the prediction. Imagine how many sets of three or four candles were placed "unconsciously," in hope.

The Voodoo That You Do

A cleaned animal's shoulder blade bone (often a mutton bone) appeared in many rituals across Europe and into Western Asia; rituals relating to this were carried out by people known as "diviners," and not all of the rituals related to love. Most importantly, to be used for divination, the bone must not have been touched by iron during the cleaning.

During one particular love-divination ritual—performed not by a diviner, but by a girl wishing to know her love's intentions—sometimes the bone was pierced with a knife or it was "borrowed" from an unmarried man, but without telling him the reason. To find out whether her current sweetheart would marry her, a girl could prick the bone with a pin nine times, over nine nights, in different places. At the end of the nine days, if his intentions were honorable, the man would come to her asking for something to cover a wound he had received during those nine days.

Plant hydrangeas near your house and your daughters will never marry.

St. Agnes's Day Fast

On St. Agnes's Day, a woman would fast until it was time to go to bed. She would then boil an egg, remove its yolk, and fill the center with salt. Afterward, she ate the entire egg, shell and all, before walking backward to bed and saying:

Sweet St. Agnes work thy fast.
If ever I be to marry man
Or man be to marry me,
I hope him this night to see.

Eating food that was more unpleasant than a hard-boiled egg filled with salt was often a part of these rituals. Another superstition required eating an entire herring, head, tails, and fins. This kind of ritual was probably undertaken to prove a person's resolve, and thereby strengthen the magic.

If a man's hat goes against the branch of a tree, someone has fallen in love with him.

Asking the Moon

Another superstition to find true love was go to a gate on the night of a new moon and ask it to reveal your lover in your dreams. Sometimes you had to make nine notches on the gate, over nine nights, before your lover's identity was disclosed.

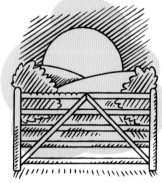

Follow the Snail Trail

As recently as the 1950s, there were reports that a snail placed in a plate of flour, or other powder, would trace the name of a future lover as it moved about—this ritual is often associated with Halloween. In some cases, the snail was even baked in the process, its dying movements producing the crucial letter.

A Hairy Situation

If you were unsuccessful in meeting, naming, or dreaming about your future partner, you could still learn something about the kind of man you would eventually find. Spinning a white-handled knife on the table was a common ritual in the twentieth century. If, when the knife stopped, the blade

Blind Bowls

In Ireland, there is an old tradition of placing three bowls in front of a fire. One contains clean water, another has dirty water, and a third is empty. Unmarried young people are blindfolded and led in the general direction of the bowls. The one they touch first determines their future: clean water for a rich partner to come; dirty water for a poor one; and the empty bowl if they are to remain single.

pointed toward you, he would be a dark-haired man. If the handle was pointing at you, he would have light hair.

Another way to find out the color of your future lover's hair was to discover a hair of the same color between your toes or in your shoe. In Wales, after hearing the first cuckoo of spring, the superstitious would remove their shoes and find a hair of the correct hue on a stocking. More generally, when you saw your first new moon of the year, if you took off your stocking and ran to the next fence along the way, you would find an indicative hair between your first and second toes.

There are numerous variations of this superstition, including one in which you must run as fast as you can—and not necessarily in a particular direction—before removing your shoe. There are others in which the hair will be found either in or under your shoe.

If a bramble clings to a girl's skirt, someone has fallen in love with her.

Plants and Plums

Young men could pull up plants, such as cabbage stalks, and tell by their size whether their future wife would be tall or short. The amount of earth around the root symbolized the size of the wife's wealth.

In one famous traditional British counting game, a woman can determine the station in life of the man she will marry by counting out cherry or prune pits, as she recites the rhyme: "Tinker, tailor, soldier, sailor. Rich man, poor man, beggar man, thief." For each pit of fruit eaten, she counts one of the above. The word you end up on reveals your future husband's station. Of course, this is an easily manipulated superstition. Many people can manage to eat only five prunes at a sitting!

Molten Lead and Egg White

Another way of divining the career of a spouse-to-be was to pour either molten lead or egg white into water. Eggs, as they were relatively easy to obtain, were usually used in this ritual. New Year's, Halloween, and Midsummer Eve (June 21st, the eve of the summer solstice) were preferred times for this ritual. The divining was very open to interpretation, and often a wise, older woman did the actual interpreting of the liquid shape. She might sit and foretell the futures of many girls in a single evening. And she undoubtedly prospered in either respect or gifts, or both—in return for a positive reading.

Fly, Ladybird, Fly

If nothing else, you could at least find out from which direction your lover would arrive. Ladybugs were instrumental

If the bread you make rises well, your sweetheart is smiling on you.

Midsummer Men

On Midsummer Eve (June 21st), the superstitious gather two stalks of a plant—usually orpine, or *Hylotelephium telephium*, a plant also known as Midsummer men because of the link with the ritual. The stalks are placed in clay, or somehow stood upright close together. Next they are given the names of two parties in a relationship and placed in a particular spot, such as above a doorway. The way they bend after being left overnight foretells the future of the couple. If the stalks bend toward each other, the two people love each other. If they remain standing upright, or bend away from each other, the couple is not in love. If the stalks bend toward each other, not only are they in love, but they also will marry within the year. In a variation on this, men from the Ozarks would test their sweetheart's love by bending a growing stalk of mullein so that it pointed toward her house. If she loved him, the mullein would grow upright again; if she loved another, it would die.

Bleeding Nose, Broken Heart

The yarrow plant was once thought to induce, as well as cure, nosebleeds. Its ambiguity was exploited by the superstitious in eastern England, who believed that one way of telling whether a love was returned involved yarrow and a brief rhyme. While tickling your nose with the plant, you would recite the following:

Yarroway, yarroway, bear a white blow
If my love love me, my nose will bleed now.

If it did, you had your proof—incontrovertible.

in this type of superstition: if one landed one your hand or you picked one up, it would fly off toward your lover. John Gay described this idea in *Shepherd's Week*:

This lady-fly I take from off the grass
Whose spotted back might scarlet red surpass
Fly, lady-bird; north, south, or east, or west
Fly where the man is found that I love best.

Sage on a Saucer

In a ritual popular in the north of England up until the nineteenth century, and particularly in the small communities and villages of rural Yorkshire, sage was used as a source of divination. In the hope of meeting their lovers, young women would gather 12 sage leaves at noon, put them on a saucer, and keep them until the following night. On each stroke of the clock at midnight, they would throw one of the leaves into the road from their open bedroom window; they believed that, on the final stroke of the clock, they would hear the step of their future husband in the street below.

Always on My Mind

A Nutty Tradition

Naturally, once a steady relationship has begun, by whatever means, people generally want to know if their partner truly loves them. Again, superstitions and rituals can help put their mind at rest—or not.

To pursue an answer, you can place two chestnuts before a fire, giving them the names of two people you know and care

Bringing Him Back If He Strays

Dragon's blood is a reddish brown resin, or powder, made from a variety of trees found around the world. Throwing it in a fire and saying a rhyme could reignite a cooling lover's interest in you. The rhyme typically followed this form:

> 'Tis not this blood I wish to burn
> But (X's) heart I wish to turn
> May he neither sleep nor rest
> Till he has granted my request.

Flinging 12 pins into a fire at midnight and a reciting a similar rhyme would have the same effect.

Another way of bringing back a lover who has lost interest was take a live pigeon, pluck out its heart, and stick pins into it. Put it under your pillow, and the lover will return. Instances of this ritual taking place were recorded in the late nineteenth century. Other animals could also be used, but the pigeon seems to have been the most popular, perhaps because it was common and therefore easy to find.

If the idea of plucking out the heart of a pigeon is too gruesome to contemplate (and why wouldn't it be), you could also burn salt at midnight and throw it into the fire while making a wish to bring back a lover who has wronged you, either to forgive him or her, or to take revenge—a much less messy proposition all round.

about. If the chestnuts burn steadily side by side, the couple will most likely marry and live a happy life together. If the nuts burst or jump away from each other, the couple will not. This experiment can also use apple seeds, peas, and plums or plum pits, depending on what is at hand and in season.

As another option, you could name two acorns, one for yourself and one for your lover. Drop both in water and, if they float close together, the two of you will marry.

Loves Me, Loves Me Not

Other well-known and popular ways of deducing the emotions of a romantic partner included plucking petals from a flower—usually a daisy—and repeating "She/he loves me" and "She/he loves me not" alternately as you remove each petal, up until the last petal is removed; the phrase accompanying it is held to be

To find out the number of sweethearts you will have, pull each finger and count the number of joints that crack.

a truth. The traditional counting rhyme "Tinker, tailor" was also used in this ritual. Or you could prick the name of the partner you wanted into a laurel leaf, place the leaf near your heart, and if the area around pricks turned pink, he or she was certain to love you. Of course, placing the leaf close to the body transferred heat to the leaf, and made it more than likely that the pricks would turn pink sooner rather than later, therefore ensuring you a hopeful, and hoped-for, outcome.

Never go courting on a Friday.

Everyday Omens

Common occurrences were frequently seen as omens. If, for example, a woman's garter came undone, her apron was untied, or her stockings were wrinkled, it was thought by some people that her lover was thinking of her, which presumably was sometimes true. On the other hand, to other superstitious people, a garter coming undone meant that a lover was being unfaithful.

Stick a crooked pin in the lining of your coat and all the girls will follow you.

Wedding-Day Wonders

Assuming that a lover was true and the couple planned to get married, they usually wanted to know when the happy day would be. As in many superstitions, cuckoos come into play here, too. The number of calls you heard was said to predict the number of years before marriage. Ladybugs could be asked directly to predict when a marriage might take place, by using a rhyme, such as:

> *Bisha-bish-barny-bee*
> *Tell me when my wedding be*
> *If it be tomorrow day*
> *Spread your wings and fly away.*

Cobwebs and Kissing

In Cornwall, England, it was said that if there are cobwebs in the house, the housemaid wants kissing. In Hampshire, England, there was an explanation for this: If the maid's beau is paying her due attention, said maid naturally holds up her head proudly and happily, and therefore notices the offending cobwebs.

On the other hand, in the Channel Islands, girls dusting their bedrooms would leave cobwebs behind on purpose because the number they saw when waking would be the amount of kisses they would receive from their fiancés.

Even if the ladybug flew, the wedding might not actually take place on the following day—particularly if that day of the week was not held to be auspicious (marrying on a Saturday, for instance, used to be frowned upon as being bad luck). The wedding would be expected, however, sooner rather than later. If the ladybug only spread its wings, and remained in place on the hand of the petitioner, a wedding was not discounted completely, but might not be as soon as hoped.

Another approach included looking at a new moon through a handkerchief or reflected in water, and counting how many moons you could see. The number corresponded to the number of years you would remain unmarried. Or you could count the number of puffs it took to blow the seeds off a dandelion to get the same result. In Lancashire, in northern England, a strange tradition grew up around Shrove Tuesday (Mardi Gras). Unmarried girls would make pancakes and feed the first, which is often said to be the worst of a batch, to a cockerel. The number of hens that joined him to eat the pancake corresponded to the number of years before the girl's wedding would take place.

Good Guess or Not?

In most parts of the world, a good guesser will never marry, especially a girl who can accurately guess the amount of each ingredient she needs for a dish she is cooking, or anyone who can accurately guess the time. In Ireland and Canada, as recently as 1923, however, the reverse was true: It was said that a good guesser would marry soon.

If you wish your love to wed, turn the bed from foot to head.

Engagement & Marriage

For many people, finding someone they love is just the beginning. Once you have snared your intended, you need to make sure you keep them firmly in your grasp, metaphorically speaking, until the marriage and beyond. There are all sorts of omens, auspices, and rituals linked with engagement and marriage, primarily designed to enhance your prospects of a long and contented union. These range from the simple notion that a groom must not see his bride before the ceremony on the day of the wedding, to more complicated—or least more difficult to arrange— signs, portents, and rituals believed to promote health, happiness, prosperity, and fruitfulness.

Meeting Mr. Right

*In earlier times, courting or dating inevitably led
to speculation about marriage—and this is often
still the case today. The longer the relationship
lasted, the more likely it would end up in
engagement and marriage. As always, there
were superstitions to be observed and events
to be avoided.*

Location, Location, Location

Where couples met was also thought to predict the success
of a relationship. Hillsides were often considered to be lucky
ground, especially if there was moving water nearby.
Therefore, near a stream or an ocean would be a good place
for luck in love. Other beliefs about lovers' meetings
included:

- To kiss for the first time by the light of a new moon
  meant the couple would soon marry, enjoy undying
  love, and never be poor.
- Lovers who met in the heart of the woods would be
  forever constant. But poplar trees brought bad luck to
  lovers.
- It was lucky if you met a black cat or a white horse
  when you were walking together.

If you are a single woman, sleeping with a
piece of wedding cake under your pillow
will bring a dream of your future husband.

Unlucky in Love

Couples had to avoid the banks of canals or ponds, bridges,
valleys, or—worst of all—crossroads. All of these places

turned love and respect into bitterness and hatred. And, frankly, they could be difficult to avoid no matter which way you turned.

Once you were at home you could try not meet or cross each other on the stairs, and it was just as bad, if not worse, if you kissed or hugged each other there. Crossing your fingers was sometimes thought to help overcome this.

No one ever really knew how long it would take for promised bad luck to arrive; superstitions are often very specific in what they foretell, but they are more vague with timescales, in some ways making their "truth" inevitable.

A spider in a bride's wedding dress brings good luck to her.

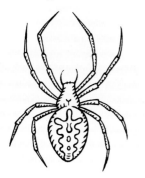

Love Letters

How you deal with letters could also influence your luck:

- Love letters must be written in either pencil or blue ink—no other shade.
- If you add kisses to the letter by writing crosses at the end, do not add four, seven, or thirteen crosses. The luckiest number is three, and it is enough to show your love. It is also unlucky to drop a letter on the way to a mailbox or to send a love letter on Christmas Day or February 29th.
- If you are writing to a sweetheart, you will have good fortune as a couple if you finish the letter while the clock is striking midnight, and you then mail the letter by the light of a full moon.

It's good luck if a cat sneezes the day before the wedding.

It's bad luck for a bride to see a pig, hare, or lizard run across the road.

Single-Girl Sense

If you are a single woman, avoid finishing a patchwork quilt on your own, without the help of others, or you will never be married. If a patchwork quilt is begun in any house, the daughters will not marry until it is finished. However, once the quilt is complete, one or more of the daughters will marry within the year.

Never give your lover a gift of gloves, a brooch, or a knife; all of these mean you will soon part, although some say that bad luck can be prevented if the receiver gives a small coin, therefore turning the gift into a purchase.

In what sounds like a modern U.S. superstition (as baseball was first played in the 1840s), it's believed that if a girl sees a bat on Valentine's Day she will marry a baseball player. And if she sees a robin, she will marry a crime fighter or a sailor.

Splitting Images

Once they are engaged, some superstitious couples will not walk together when leaving another person's wedding, fearing they will soon part. It is also common for an engaged couple to refuse to be photographed together, which is also said to cause a split or mean that the marriage will be unhappy.

These superstitions may be related to the belief that the reflection in a glass lens or a printed image might capture a person's spirit. It is also considered unlucky for a couple to look together at a new moon through glass.

When a girl hears a cock crow while thinking of her lover, however, it means she will be married soon.

If a bride meets a funeral, monk, or nun, she can expect bad luck.

Engaging Manners for Men

Men are often told that an offer of marriage is best made on a Friday evening, and if it is accepted, they can announce the engagement the following day. However, a man making a proposal may be turned down if his family name and her maiden name begin with the same letter, as is noted in this American rhyme from 1853:

Change the name but not the letter,
Change for the worse and not for the better.

Luckily this problem is less frequent these days because more women are choosing to keep their names.

Proposers must wear something blue because this is the luckiest color for lovers. Jewels containing any turquoise are also a good gift for this reason.

Sixpence Seals It

In a tradition dating from the time of England's Elizabeth I, sixpence coins have long been associated with weddings. Originally, a bride would often receive a silver sixpence as a wedding gift. Gradually the custom evolved until the sixpence came to be seen as a lucky charm by the Victorians, ensuring the happiness and longevity of the marriage.

Meeting a monk or nun on your wedding day means the marriage will be barren.

Half but Whole

Sharing the halves of a sixpence, which is lucky in itself, proves a couple's faith and ensures that they will never part. Keeping a lock of the other person's hair will also do the same. In Victorian times, lockets were made for this very purpose, and women often kept a picture of their loved one in one half and a lock of his hair in the other. This long-lived tradition is still carried out today, even if more from sentimentality than superstition.

The Calendar Counts

Choosing the Day

According to superstition, these are good days and bad days for weddings. June is said to be the luckiest. This may be due to the likelihood of good weather if you live in the northern hemisphere, as acknowledged by the English saying:

Happy is the bride the sun shines on.

In Poland, it is lucky to be married in any month with the letter "r" in it, which means only six of the 12 months. This tradition may bring good fortune to the couple, but it's very unlucky for wedding singers!

May is also an unpopular wedding month among the superstitious. The beliefs about May and June may be related to the ancient Roman names for the months, which were named after the goddesses Maia and Juno. Maia was the consort of Vulcan, who controlled the fiery elements, and this association with tempestuousness is thought to encourage great disharmony in a marriage. Juno, the devoted wife of Jupiter, is said to be responsible for women's lives—just the kind of attention you need on your wedding day.

Wednesday is often said to be the most auspicious day for a wedding. Two rhymes commonly used to help a couple pick their wedding day are:

Monday for wealth,
Tuesday for health,
Wednesday the best day of all.
Thursday for crosses,
Friday for losses,
Saturday no luck at all.

Marry when the year is new, he will be loving,
  kind and true.
When February birds do mate,
  you wed nor dread your fate.
If you wed when March winds blow,
  joy and sorrow both you will know.
Marry in April if you can, joy for maiden and
  for man.
Marry in the month of May, you will surely rue
  the day.
Marry when June roses grow and over land
  and sea you will go.
Those who in July do wed must labour
  for their daily bread.
Whoever wed in August be,
  many a change is sure to see.
Marry in September's shine,
  your loving will be rich and fine.
If in October you do marry,
  love will come but riches tarry.
If you wed in bleak November,
  only joy will come, remember.
When December's snows fall fast,
  marry and true love will last.

Shades of Luck

All around the world people get married dressed in different colors considered to be lucky. In India, red and gold are traditionally thought to be favorable; red stands for happiness, while gold represents fortune.

The traditional white wedding in the Western and/or Christian world is actually a recent idea. Until the second half of the nineteenth century, white was just one of many colors thought suitable for weddings. Even in the early twentieth century there was a rhyme to help brides decide what was right for the big day:

> *Married in white, you have chosen all right*
> *Married in gray, you will go far away*
> *Married in black, you will wish yourself back*
> *Married in red, you will wish yourself dead*
> *Married in green, ashamed to be seen*
> *Married in blue, you'll always be true*
> *Married in pearl, you'll live in a whirl*
> *Married in yellow, ashamed of the fellow*
> *Married in brown, you'll live out of town*
> *Married in pink, your spirits will sink.*

Perhaps the most common wedding-day superstition is:

> *Something old, something new,*
> *something borrowed, something blue.*

There is an extra line: "And a lucky sixpence in her shoe," arising from the English tradition of giving a sixpence as a bridal gift. The old item was traditionally shoes, and everything else was usually new. It is also thought lucky if the borrowed item is a veil worn by a bride who has a happy marriage.

Blue is seen as the hue of love, as it represents constancy and fidelity, and is usually worn as a decorative garter. Many people believe that the bride should never help to make her dress. It is very unlucky to tear the dress on the wedding day, or to spill blood on it—highly likely when it was held together with pins.

If you didn't care for your prospects in that rhyme, you could always turn to this one:

> *Married in January's roar and rime,*
> *Widowed you'll be before your prime*
> *Married in February's sleepy weather,*
> *Life you'll tread in time together*
> *Married when March winds shrill and roar,*
> *Your home will lie on a distant shore*
> *Married 'neath April's changeful skies,*
> *A chequered path before you lies*
> *Married when bees o'er May blossoms flit,*
> *Strangers around your board will sit*
> *Married in month of roses June,*
> *Life will be one long honeymoon*
> *Married in July with flowers ablaze,*
> *Bittersweet memories in after days*
> *Married in August's heat and drowse,*
> *Lover and friend in your chosen spouse*
> *Married in September's golden glow,*
> *Smooth and serene your life will go*
> *Married when leaves in October thin,*
> *Toil and hardships for you begin*
> *Married in veils of November mist,*
> *Fortune your wedding ring has kissed*
> *Married in days of December's cheer,*
> *Love's star shines brighter from year to year.*

When practicality comes into play, weekend days are often chosen. Plan to marry when the new moon is just beginning to wax, however, and luck will be on your side.

Even the time of day is important. Some people believe that if a wedding takes place as the hand on a clock is moving upward, the marriage will be a lucky one; if the hand is ticking downward, it's unlucky.

From This Day Forth

Veil of Pearls

The tradition for a bride to wear a veil probably originated in the East. It may be a relic of the purdah custom practiced by Hindus and Muslims that forbade a man to look at a woman's face until she was married. Or perhaps it is derived from the canopy held over the heads of the happy couple as part of the ceremony. A canopy still plays a part in Jewish weddings, and in China an umbrella is often held over the bride and groom. Another theory is that a veil protects the

If you dream of pearls, you will have a very successful marriage or business venture.

Pins

Pins were once used to hold all types of clothes together, so they were considered valuable items and were often quite intricately wrought. It was also thought lucky to find and pick up a pin, and bad luck to see one on the ground and not pick it up.

See a pin and pick it up
And all day long
You'll have good luck

At one time, the pins from a bride's wedding dress were thought to possess special powers, but there is some disagreement on whether they bring good or bad luck. Still, it was once a common belief that a pin from a bride's gown would bring a wedding for its new owner, and therefore a bride might allow certain friends to take a pin each out of her dress. It is a long-held superstition; supposedly when Mary Queen of Scots was married in 1565, she allowed every man that could approach her to take a pin from her dress.

Ringing In Some Changes

The powerful symbolism of a wedding ring is only one of the beliefs associated with wearing rings. Rings can also relay messages to the public, including:

- Men and women who wear a ring on the first finger of the left hand want to be married.

- A ring on the second finger means that the wearer prefers friendship to romance.

- A third-finger ring means the person is engaged to be married.

- A fourth-, or little-, finger ring means that the person has no intention to marry.

An engaged woman should not allow another woman to try on her engagement ring, and brides and grooms should not try on their wedding rings before the ceremony; the result could be an end to the engagement or an unhappy married life.

To lose a wedding or an engagement ring signifies a break-up to come; this is why many people never take off their wedding rings. But if a wife does remove her wedding ring, there will be no bad luck if the husband puts it back on for her.

If a wedding ring is dropped during the ceremony, the marriage will be unhappy. This is based on the superstitious belief that a bad start does not bode well for the rest of the relationship. Some people think the person who drops the ring will die before the other.

bride from the evil eye, or ever-present evil spirits. Some people also believe that bridesmaids are dressed much like the bride so that any evil spirits will be confused and not know which maiden to target. Similarly, the groomsmen would be dressed like the groom.

According to some, pearls are not to be worn as part of a bridal outfit—according to legend, pearls bring tears. They are suitable wedding gifts, however, as they symbolize purity and innocence. A bride's father traditionally gives her pearls. This may have originated in the Indian *Rigveda*, which dates back to about 1000 B.C. Krishna is said to have brought pearls from the sea for his daughter on her wedding day. Brides often give pearls as presents to their bridesmaids, too.

> If a stone rolls across the path of a newly married couple, bad luck will follow.

A Shoe-in

In Poland, a girl places her shoes on the windowsill the day before her wedding to ensure she will have good weather on the day. She can't look at her reflection in the mirror when she is completely dressed, or she will have bad luck. And if she wants to be the decision maker in the marriage, she needs to drape some of the fabric of her dress over her new husband's shoe to bring this about.

Sweeping Beliefs

In Britain, touching or seeing a chimney sweep on a wedding day is considered to be very fortunate, for either the bride or the groom. In some superstitions, the bride might have to kiss the sweep to get her luck, being careful of soot, of course.

Prince Philip, the Duke of Edinburgh, was delighted to find a sweep in the street on his 1947 wedding day to the future queen Elizabeth II. Chimney sweeps were already becoming less common, so the sweep may have been seen by design rather than by accident. Working chimney sweeps still exist, even though many people use central heating instead of fireplaces. Now they can earn as much, if not more, from a roaring trade in wedding appearances as they do sweeping chimneys.

In much of the world, the groom is not allowed to see the bride in her wedding dress until the wedding. But there is a certain amount of logic in this because a girl's wedding outfit is likely to be one of the best she'll ever wear—and on this day she'll want to make an impression.

In Sweden, it is traditional for a bride to put a handful of earth from her home in her weddings shoes, so that she will never be homesick and start her marriage on a positive note.

The Day of Bells and Roses

There are good and bad omens to look for even when the big day arrives.

- It is unlucky for the car to turn around immediately after dropping the bride at the ceremony. Superstitious chauffeurs will drive a little farther before turning, or take a route that avoids returning the way they came.

Self-Help Luck

Storks have long been associated with love and fidelity because they mate for life; when one dies, the other never takes another partner.

In northern Europe, storks commonly nest on top of chimneys. They are thought to protect the house against fire and lightning, as well as confer domestic bliss on the occupants. This belief was so strong that, when storks began recently to disappear from large parts of the region, people mounted huge campaigns to bring them back. Communities in many areas cooperated to legislate tighter pollution control, lower telephone cables to make flying safer, and design buildings with chimneys especially suited for storks. The campaigns worked: The stork population is on the rise again, and many people are happier. Sometimes you simply have to make good luck happen.

- It is bad luck if church bells ring during the ceremony. It could possibly mean the death of the bride or groom. Some brides will wait outside until the bells stop.
- It is believed to be very good luck for the bride to cry copiously on her wedding day, so that she will cry very little in her married life.

Orange Blossom

The orange blossom has been associated with weddings for centuries.

In the Middle Ages, Saracen brides in the Eastern Mediterranean wore a wreath of orange blossoms over their wedding veils, and it is likely that this custom was introduced to the West by Crusaders returning from fighting the Saracens. The superstition behind the custom probably began because the orange tree is evergreen and could be relied on during the winter.

The evergreen also symbolizes a couple's everlasting love and, because the orange tree is one of the very few that bears blossom and fruit at the same time, it might have been symbolic of the hoped-for fertility of the couple. It certainly worked for Queen Victoria, who was married with an orange blossom in her hair and went on to have nine children. The symbolism of the orange blossom may have originated even further East. The ancient Chinese believed the flowers to be both lucky and symbolic of the purity and innocence of the bride.

Real orange blossoms were very expensive, and only the rich could afford them. Inevitably, therefore, they wilted and were discarded. Fake orange blossoms worn by the less affluent were also thrown away after a month or so. Orange blossoms, real or fake, are still worn by brides and are often one of the few souvenirs of the headpiece or bouquet that is kept.

Meeting an elephant on the way to one's wedding is very lucky indeed, and bodes extremely well for the marriage.

Let the Party Begin

Breaking Up Is Good to Do

Breaking a glass is an important part of the Jewish wedding ritual. After the bride and groom drink from a special glass, it is dropped to the floor and the groom steps on it with his right foot, smashing it to pieces. It is said to symbolize the Romans' destruction of the Temple of Jerusalem in A.D. 70, which must never be forgotten—even in the happiest of times.

In Germany, it is said that if the groom buckles the bride's left shoe on their wedding day, she will take control in the marriage.

First Gift, First Job

To avoid bad luck, the first gift opened by the bride must also be the first one that she uses. It is also believed that the person who gave the third gift opened at a wedding shower will soon have a baby. For the Chinese, mandarin ducks symbolize marital happiness; they often appear on wedding gifts such as pillowcases, bedcovers, and handkerchiefs.

Who's the Boss?

There are several superstitions about who will take control in the marriage, and they are often based on which of the partners does something first. This includes stepping out of

Catch Me If You Can

The popular custom of a bride throwing her bouquet to her bridesmaids, in the belief that whomever catches it would be the next to be married, is relatively new and it originated in the United States. In France, the bride throws her garter instead of her bouquet, whereas today in the United States and elsewhere, the garter is often ceremonially removed by the groom and thrown to the bachelors among the wedding guests.

Other customs associated with the bride's flowers and wedding dress include the breaking up of the bouquet. A single flower from a bride's bouquet was traditionally thought to be lucky, so brides often divided up their bouquets and gave flowers to their friends, to pass along good luck and happiness.

The most traditional item to be thrown was a stocking (and relates to today's ritual of throwing a garter). The tradition was originally carried out in a variety of ways, by both men and women. For example, a high point of the wedding day—before honeymoons became common—was putting the bride and groom to bed in their bedchamber. This involved an amount of fun and ribaldry, depending on the people involved, but throwing a stocking was always a fairly standard part of the activity. Other stocking traditions included:

- The bride would throw her left stocking over her right shoulder, and the person hit was to be the next married.

- Guests threw their left stocking over their right shoulder with the left hand, hoping to hit the bride or groom in the face.

- Only unmarried guests could take turns, with the men throwing the bride's stocking and the women throwing the man's stocking. If any of them scored a hit, they were soon to be married.

- In a German variation, when the bride is undressing for bed, she gives one of her stockings to a bridesmaid. The bridesmaid then throws the stocking toward the crowd of guests and whomever it lands on will be the next to marry.

the church first or into the marital home. This may be the reasoning behind the groom carrying his bride over the threshold. If the bride and groom both plant a sage bush, the one whose sage grows tallest will be the dominant partner in the marriage.

Similar superstitions relate to which of the two will die first, but there is little agreement about what means what; it is variously believed the first to kneel, stand up, turn away from the altar, or even speak the loudest will be the first to die.

A German couple may also compete to stomp on the other's feet, whoever manages it first being the one who will retain mastery over the other.

Mooning Around

The word "honeymoon" may have originated with drinking mead, a beverage made from honey; ancient Teutonic races associated mead with festivity. Or, it may be an ironic reference to the full moon as a symbol of sweetness. The moon is no sooner full than it begins to wane—possibly similar to the period of intense affection after a marriage that may last as little as a month. The term "honeymoon" was used in this sense as early as the sixteenth century; it  wasn't until the early nineteenth century that it meant a time when a couple traveled for pleasure. In North America, Niagara Falls was long a popular destination for honeymooning couples, a tradition said to have been started by Napoleon Bonaparte's younger brother, Jerome, who went there with his American bride, Elizabeth Patterson. Today, many couples throw pennies into Niagara's Bridal Veil Falls, for good luck.

If a dog runs between the newly married couple it signifies bad luck to come.

Hitting the Spot

Throwing something at the bride and groom for luck is an old wedding tradition, known since at least the fifteenth century. It may date back even further to the ancient Romans and Egyptians. Wheat was probably the most common missile until the late nineteenth century, when rice became more traditional, particularly in the United States. Indeed, in France, wheat is still often thrown, to symbolize abundance.

Victorian folklorists sometimes interpreted the throwing as a fertility gesture, but there is no evidence to support this. Some say the rice is intended to distract and feed any evil spirits who had come to disrupt the marriage. Today, we throw paper confetti, birdseed, or even flower petals or dried lavender.

Named after the sugared almonds and candy thrown at Italian weddings (and in similar pastel colors), confetti is often cut into such "good luck" symbols as horseshoes.

Shivaree Sounds

Even today in some parts of the United States, a shivaree—where bells, horns, pots and pans, or other noisy things are clanged to "serenade" the newlyweds—is held to welcome the bride and groom to their marriage bed.

This tradition is thought to have been brought to the United States by French settlers and traders who made their new home around and along the Mississippi River and it was a common practice by the early nineteenth century.

Fertility

Superstitious beliefs often filled the gaps when people lacked knowledge about or answers to some situations. Fertility in people, plants, and animals was often a misunderstood subject. Superstitions appeared to provide some control over the unknown, and were readily fostered in response to the very human need need to try to ensure the best possible outcome when it came to bearing children, growing crops, and husbanding animals. In a time when there there was little in the way of scientific knowledge and certainly no modern medicine, the world of superstition and ritual was seen as a way to try to control the vagaries of the natural world. After all, lives depended on bountiful harvests and healthy livestock. With the mystery surrounding fertility in humans, and the dangers attached to childbirth itself, it is perhaps not surprising that people also turned to magic, signs, and omens to better their chances of conceiving.

Potent Predictions

Traditional magic and rituals were practiced all over the world in an attempt to control nature to people's advantage.

Singing for Apples

Wassailing is typically known as the tradition of going from one house to another, singing carols and eating, drinking, and socializing. Originally, it grew out of an English fertility ritual that usually took place in orchards, and particularly apple orchards. The term "wassailing" comes from the Anglo-Saxon *wæs hæil* ("Be healthy"), but its origins extend back even further in English history. The participants make toasts or salutations to the relatively dormant trees in winter so that they would have strong crops the following spring. Apple cider or another alcoholic beverage would be sprinkled at the trees' roots, and rhymes were said, such as:

> *Here's to thee old apple tree*
> *Hats full, sacks full*
> *Great bushel baskets full.*
> *Hurrah!*

Guns were sometimes fired to frighten away evil spirits, and people danced around the trees before moving on to the next orchard. In England's West Country, it was believed that if children were allowed to "steal" the remaining fruit from apple trees after harvesting, the following year's crop would be better. This was called the "piskies' harvest."

Pleading for the Trees

In Romania, people make a *turta*, a traditional Christmas confection that has many layers of pastry, and is filled with melted sugar, honey, and ground walnuts or hemp seed. When the wife is in the middle of kneading the dough, she follows

her husband into the garden. The man goes to each tree that has not been fruitful that year, threatening to cut the tree down. Each time, the wife begs him to spare the tree, saying:

Oh no, I am sure that this tree will be as heavy with fruit next spring as are my fingers with dough this day.

Winter Greenery

In Germany, people brought boughs of evergreen trees into their homes in the winter months because these were thought to protect the home and ensure that life would return in the spring. This may have been the origin of the modern-day Christmas tree.

A Calming Influence

Some superstitious farmers still keep a donkey or goat in a field with cattle. It is said to calm the cattle down, or bring good luck, and that it ensures fertility among the cattle.

Lucky 13

Interestingly, in a belief perhaps stemming from the Romans' view that the gods rejoiced in uneven numbers, it was once customary to set a hen on an odd number of eggs, as it was believed an even number would hatch only male chicks, which would not produce eggs. In France, the ideal number was 13, perhaps to allow for the even dozen if one did not hatch.

If you eat both kernels of a double-kerneled nut, you will have twins.

A Good Year for Nuts

In the past, it was common for people to explain the events in human lives by creating a superstition that linked with occurrences in the natural world. In Britain, it was commonly said that a good year for nuts was a good one for babies—in reality, it was often the following year. One source, *Poor*

Waxing and Waning

The gravitational pull of the moon influences the Earth by causing tides and, anecdotally, generally affecting people's moods and women's menstrual cycles. So it seems entirely logical that people should follow the phases of the moon to decide the best time for planting and harvesting.

The Greeks, Chinese, and Romans were all guided by the lunar calendar when it came to planting and harvesting. So, too, the Maoris of New Zealand and tribes in Central America. Indeed, "lunar planting" is a phenomenon that can be found pretty much around the world, and many people still follow its precepts today. According to long-held and widespread tradition, food that grows below ground, such as potatoes and carrots, needs to be planted during a waning moon. Food that grows above the ground, such as green vegetables, should be planted during a waxing moon. Fruit trees should be grafted three or four days before a waxing moon, which is said to give the tree time to prepare to bear its fruit.

Most beliefs that plants and animals had a connection with the moon go back to ancient origins, as they appear consistently in literature in many countries and throughout the ages from classical to recent times.

For centuries people timed the lives or deaths of their animals by the state of the moon, too. Pigs were often killed at home rather than at professional butchers, so many recorded beliefs are about pigs. It was once thought that meat from a pig killed during the waning of the moon would either weigh less to begin with or would shrink during cooking. On the other hand, meat from a pig killed during the waxing of the moon—ideally close to a full moon—would weigh more. In fact, that it might even become plumper when cooked.

Traditionally, lambs' tails were never docked when the moon was on the wane, in fear that the lambs would die as a result. Male lambs were gelded, however, when the moon was waning, a few days past full.

In North America, the early Algonquin tribes kept track of passing time in the year by naming each full moon. The harvest moon is the one that falls in September or, in some years, October. For the few nights each side of the full harvest moon, farmers could work late into the night harvesting the many crops that were ready for gathering, including corn, squash, beans, and wild rice.

Mistletoe

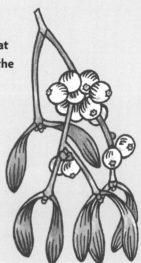

Mistletoe has a long association with fertility, and kissing under it at Christmas is a common tradition. It was once believed to increase the likelihood of love and/or marriage in the coming year. During the Middle Ages, it was thought to possess both aphrodisiac and fertility-inducing properties, and women who wanted to conceive might wrap their wrists and waists with bunches of mistletoe. Mistletoe berries or leaves were sometimes prescribed as a cure for women unable to have children—either by carrying the leaves around in a pouch, or by ingesting the berries. It was also thought in some places that a good crop of mistletoe foretold a good crop for the farmers the following year.

Mistletoe is a semi-parasitic plant that grows on the surface of several kinds of trees. Its name is derived from Germanic languages and means "dung twig," or a plant that grows from dung, because birds would eat the berries and pass the seed in their droppings to propagate the plants. To simple folk, the plant seemed to spring magically out of the droppings. Mistletoe also remains green throughout the winter, even though the deciduous tree it grows on appears to be dead, which makes it a powerful symbol of fertility. In the European species, the branches and leaves grow in pairs, and the berry contains a white sticky juice—all of which help link it to human sexuality and love.

Mistletoe also held a role in Norse mythology. According to legend, Balder was the son of Odin and Frigg, and the most beloved of the gods. He dreamed of his own imminent death and, to protect him, his mother made everything that sprang from the four elements—air, water, fire, and earth—swear an oath not to harm him. The other gods enjoyed Balder's immunity to harm, and played games where they tried to kill him in various ways, only to watch him recover. Mistletoe was accidentally left off Frigg's list, however, and Loki, an evil god who was jealous of Balder, soon found out. He made an arrow out of mistletoe and gave it to Hoder, Balder's brother, who was blind. Guiding Hoder's hand, Loki pointed the arrow at Balder's heart. Hoder shot the arrow and Balder was killed. Frigg's tears were said to have turned into the white berries of the mistletoe. In another version, after three days Balder was restored to life, and Frigg made the mistletoe a symbol of love. In Scandinavia, warring parties who happened to meet under mistletoe would have a day of peace, or warring spouses would kiss and make up.

It is believed that druid elders collected sprigs of mistletoe with a golden sickle, usually under a waxing moon, using a cloth to catch it as it fell to make sure it never touched the ground. The most sacred mistletoe was found growing on an oak tree. While the druids used mistletoe as magical protection, they fed it to cattle to ensure their fertility.

The ancient Romans had a similar use for mistletoe. To keep Saturn, the god of seedtime and harvest, happy, they held a seven-day festival called Saturnalia. Part of the festivities included kissing and other fertility rituals under the mistletoe.

If you want to observe traditional etiquette when kissing under the mistletoe, the man should pluck a berry from it each time he kisses a woman; when there are no berries left, the kissing can cease.

Robin's Almanack of 1668, provides a possible explanation:

> ... *many a poor country labouring man may be horrified this month, when their wives go into the wood, picking of nuts, for opportunity has been the occasion of making many a man a cuckold.*

This passage can also explain why "nutting" is an old euphemism for sexual intercourse.

Single women would burn old mistletoe to predict their marriage prospects: Steady flames meant a happy union.

Making Babies

Plants and Pregnancy

There are a few connections in traditional beliefs between parsley and pregnancy. In Britain, it was said that if a young woman sowed parsley seed or picked parsley, she would soon become pregnant. On the other hand, in some areas parsley was thought to prevent or abort pregnancy. There is some basis for this. Parsley can stimulate menstruation and produce contractions in the uterus—but only if a woman eats a truly prodigious amount of parsley, far more than in the average garnish. A similar set of beliefs existed around lettuce.

Mandrake was believed to be both an aphrodisiac and a fertility enhancer. This belief may derive from its roots, which often branch into two at the bottom and grow out at the sides, therefore resembling the human form. Arabic people used both the fruit and root of the mandrake as an aphrodisiac, and called it the "servant of love."

If a pregnant woman puts two spoons
in a saucer, she will have red-haired twins.

All around the Maypole

Most people around the world, particularly in the northern hemisphere, are familiar with May Day, which originated as a European festival to celebrate the first planting of spring and encourage the Earth and nature in general to reproduce and be fertile. Celts and Saxons celebrated May 1st as Beltane, or day of fire. Bel was god of the sun, and they welcomed the return of the sun after winter with fires and torches.

The maypole, which we connect to May Day today, was originally a simple phallic symbol; erecting it was an equally important part of the ritual as dancing round it. The ribbons that are involved in the dance are a more recent addition, as are Morris dancing and children dancing round the maypole. These gradually became part of the celebrations as May Day drew further away from its pre-Christian pagan roots. Also, on May Day Eve, young men and women often went out to collect green boughs and blossoms to symbolize the rebirth of spring, though this may have been an excuse to find a private place for more intimate pursuits. Certainly, the Puritans of seventeenth-century England didn't approve, and called for the banning of all maypoles. May Day celebrations still take place around the world, especially in Britain, Germany, and the United States, and have undergone a revival since the recent resurgence of interest in and practice of paganism.

Dream of a black-and-white cat and you'll soon have children.

Barren Fields

In Germany, it is sometimes said that if a woman walks over a garden bed or field within six weeks of having a baby, either everything will die or nothing will grow on it for the next few years. In Uganda, a barren woman is said to cause an infertile garden, and her husband is entitled to petition for a divorce on the grounds that this will cause the couple undue economic difficulties.

In Britain, one way to cure infertility was to go outside naked into your garden on Midsummer's Eve (June 21st, the eve of the summer solstice) and pick the herb known as Saint John's Wort. We now know that this contains an antidepressant, so it may have helped to lift moods and increase sexual relations.

Throwing rice at a newlywed couple transfers the power of the Earth's fertility to them.

If a girl leaps over a broom, she will soon be pregnant.

Eggs-ellent Superstition

Eggs as a representation of fertility also hold a place in rituals to have children. If a superstitious Jewish woman in a childless couple finds a double-yolked egg and eats it, she may well believe that she will have many children.

If a Russian Jewish bride-to-be wants to have children, she can choose to carry an egg in her bosom on her way to the *chuppah*, the canopy under which the bride and groom stand during the wedding ceremony. In Asia, meanwhile, a bride who steps over fish roe (eggs) will have many healthy babies.

Sitting and Sleeping

For at least the second half of the twentieth century, and probably before that, it was a commonly touted old wives' tale that if a woman sat on a chair just after a pregnant woman had left it, she would soon become pregnant, too. The same belief could be applied to the bed in which a baby had recently been born.

On the other hand, in Russia, traditional superstition states that sitting on a cold surface, such as on a rock or on the ground, will inhibit a woman's ability to have children.

In Ireland, women who had failed to have children once believed that sleeping for a night on one of the stone megaliths known as Diarmuid's Bed or Graine's Bed would help them to become pregnant. Holed stones, such as the one at Glencolmcille in County Donegal, were also used, and other stones and even wells engendered the same belief.

Lupercalia

Every February, just before the advent of spring, the ancient Romans celebrated a festival called Lupercalia, which was held to keep evil spirits at bay, purify the city of Rome, and bring fertility. The event celebrated the story of Romulus and Remus. These twin brothers were said to have been cast out into the wild as infants when the throne of their grandfather, King of Alba Longa, was usurped by his brother. The little boys survived thanks to a she-wolf that suckled and cared for them until a shepherd and his wife found the boys and raised them. When the twins reached manhood, they defeated the usurper king and restored their grandfather to the throne. Next, growing bored with their lives, they decided to build their own city, and they chose the place where the wolf had nursed them, by the banks of the River Tiber. They argued, however, over who was more favored by the gods and should therefore be in charge of the city, and Romulus killed his brother. He went on to found Rome, which he named after himself.

During Lupercalia—which undoubtedly changed over time, as Christian beliefs became more prevalent and pagan rites were increasingly outlawed—young men sacrificed, for example, one or two goats and a dog. Two of the young men, possibly in reference to human sacrifice made in earlier versions, were marked on the forehead with the blood of the victims, then wiped clean with cloth dipped in milk. Next, they made loincloths and cut small strips out of the skin of the sacrificed goat. Wearing the loincloths and carrying the strips, they ran around Palatine Hill, the site where Rome was said to be have been founded. As they ran, they struck women and girls with the strips of goatskin to promote fertility, prevent barrenness, and ease the pains of childbirth. The strips were called "februa"—the Latin term *februum*, which means "purification," is the basis of the name for the month of February. By the fifth century, celebration of Lupercalia had been banned completely.

Babies
& Children

Parents throughout the ages have taken great pains to keep their children safe and healthy. As with most things in life, these steps have given rise to an array of superstitions. Many doctors, midwives, and parents can report interesting rituals and practices designed to protect newborns and babies. While many of these arose at a time when childbirth was a precarious business and infant mortality was high, a surprising number still persist. Some include dressing infants in certain clothes, putting them through various rituals, and giving them special gifts to bring good luck.

Newborn Hopes

Whether wanting to ensure a healthy baby, wishing to influence the baby's gender, or seeking to keep any evil spirits at bay from a newborn child, the superstitious person can choose from a wealth of omens, rituals, and practices.

And Along Came Baby

Finding a hollow loaf of bread was sometimes believed to foretell a birth. Although not a prediction of pregnancy, a shooting star was also seen as a sign that a new baby had been born, and the star was the newborn's soul arriving to join the baby on Earth. This may, however, just have been a story invented for children to postpone telling them the true facts of life. Another omen that predicted an upcoming birth was an oval-shaped cinder bouncing out of the fire.

Boy or Girl?

A widespread traditional way to predict the sex of a baby was to dangle a wedding ring or needle by a hair or thread over the pregnant woman's stomach, and watch how it moved. When it was dangled, it would move either in a circle or from side to side. If the ring swings like a pendulum, the baby will be a girl; if it swings in a circle, it will be a boy…or is that the other way around? Unfortunately, there seems to be no agreement as to which movement foretold which gender.

If you tickle a baby's feet, it will grow up with a stammer.

In Korea, to guarantee a boy, the woman is advised before conceiving to pray to various divinities, such as those found in trees and rocks, and the stars in the constellation known as

the Great Bear—also known as the Plough. Once she is pregnant, if the woman dreams of fierce animals, the child will be a boy. The child will be a girl if she dreams of flowers or other feminine things. In China, it is believed that a woman should eat carrots, lettuce, mushrooms, and tofu seven days before conception if she wants to have a boy; for a girl, it's fish, meat, and pickles.

Pass the Salt

In Scotland, a newborn baby was bathed in salt water, and had to taste the water three times to protect it against the

The Chinese believe that if an expectant mother rubs her belly too much, her child may be born spoiled.

Dress for Success

In past times, some nurses and midwives dressed newborn babies in old clothes rather than new ones, and often they used the clothes of someone of the opposite sex. For example, a baby girl might be wrapped her father's shirt. This may have been done to confuse any fairies or evil spirits looking for babies to steal, but it was also said to ensure that when the baby grew up, it would be attractive to people of the opposite sex.

There are also superstitions about when it was a good time to dress babies in particular types of clothing. For example, a rhyme from Cornwall, England, says: "Tuck babies in May, you'll tuck them away." "Tucking" meant dressing children in short clothes. A good time to both wean babies and dress them in spring clothing was Good Friday, considered a lucky day in many other ways, too.

Baby's First Mouthful

In the late nineteenth century in Yorkshire, England, babies were often given a teaspoonful of butter and sugar as their first food. This is most likely taken from the following biblical passage:

> *Behold, a virgin shall conceive, and bear a son, and shall call his name Immanuel. Butter and honey shall he eat, that he may know to refuse the evil, and choose the good (Isaiah 7:15).*

Presumably it was thought that butter and sugar—which was probably more commonly in the house than honey at certain times of the year—would produce a similar effect in the child, and that he or she would refuse evil and choose good.

evil eye. Salt, which is a good antiseptic, is also a symbol of purity and incorruptibility because of its preserving qualities. And three is a very lucky number, which here may relate to any set of relevant trinities, such as the Christian holy trinity (God the Father, Son, and Holy Spirit), the three graces (faith, hope, and charity), and the threefold nature of man (mind, body, and spirit). In traditions ranging from Ireland to Italy, salt was sometimes placed in a baby's cradle to ward off witchcraft.

Babies were said to have particular characteristics depending on the day of the week they were born. In the

In Ireland, a little salt was tied up in a baby's clothing at bedtime to act as a talisman to keep the fairies away.

Tempting Fate

The ancient Greeks believed in three Parcae, or Fates, who controlled all human lives from birth to death. They were were cruel and had no regard for anyone's wishes. Today, we habitually refer to this ancient Greek belief when we remark that it is possible to "tempt fate." This is the idea that, if we make a certain decision or carry out a particular action to make something happen, fate will step in and reverse our wishes or efforts.

This kind of idea is demonstrated in a superstition that says that when a woman gives away all of her babies' clothes, she will very soon be pregnant again. The belief also appears in an early twentieth century superstitions, where people avoided measuring or weighing a baby because it thought that this would somehow tempt fate to make the baby die, or at least become sick or stunt its growth. Unfortunately, this sentiment may also be a macabre reference to measuring the baby for a coffin. Stepping over a child's head was also once thought to stunt its growth. And you had to be careful when you chose to knit. Knitting clothes for a baby before its birth was seriously tempting fate. Fate was thought to ensure that the baby either grew up a sick child or was miscarried.

According to German superstition, during pregnancy fate can be tempted in a number of ways. Many of the following examples have spread to other countries around the world:

- If a pregnant woman ties a rope around her waist instead of a belt, her child will be hanged.

- If she woman walks behind or crosses the path of a criminal who is condemned to death, her child will suffer the same fate.

- If a pregnant women is eating bread, it's important not to pierce it with a knife or fork—as this may poke out the child's eyes.

- If she goes anywhere where cloth is being bleached, her child will be pale.

- To guarantee an easy labor, a pregnant woman should turn over the tub she has used for washing the clothes after doing the laundry. And ideally her husband will tie her garters and lend her his slippers to wear.

United Kingdom, many people can still recite this common 1838 rhyme:

Monday's child is fair of face
Tuesday's child is full of grace
Wednesday's child is full of woe
Thursday's child has far to go
Friday's child is loving and giving
Saturday's child works hard for a living
But the child that is born on the Sabbath day
Is bonny and blithe and good and gay.

There are variations of the rhyme, some of which begin on a Sunday. Other superstitions assign different traits to the days. There was, however, an overall strongly held belief that the day of birth was important.

In fact, astrology can be a strong influence on someone's lifestyle decisions. For example, in Chinese astrology, there are 12 animals that each correspond to a year. There are also five elements matched to the animals. This results in a 60-year cycle with various underlying annual attributes and levels of auspiciousness. In Japan, where the Chinese system is also adopted among the superstitious, a "fire horse" year is unlucky for having baby girls. Girls born in this year are said to be headstrong, independent, and ambitious, and none of these traits was traditionally attractive in Japanese culture. In 1966, the last fire horse year, records show that birth rates dipped by about half a million in comparison with the previous and following years because many women did not want to have children who might have trouble finding a spouse.

Born on a Sunday, you're a tyrant all your life.

Timing was important, too. People born at night were said to be unfortunate or to have the ability to see ghosts and visions. People born during the day would never see ghosts or visions. Babies born at midnight were said to be psychic.

This was especially the case for those born at midnight on certain special nights, such as Christmas Eve or Halloween.

According to some superstitions, other conditions at the time of birth would also have a bearing on a child's future. A child born during a storm would have a troublesome life, but one born when the moon was waxing would have good luck. A baby born when the moon was new would be eloquent. Girls born when the moon was waxing would be precocious. If a boy was born on a waning moon, the next child would be a girl, and vice versa.

In Indonesia, carrying a pair of scissors at all times will protect a pregnant woman and her baby from possible evil and harm.

Meeting and Greeting

In the past, a superstitious Christian mother would not bring her baby to visit anyone until it had been christened. Once she did take the baby out, she would most likely choose to visit someone with a pleasant disposition because it was believed that the temper of the first person to kiss the baby would be conferred upon the child. Whenever a baby first visited, or when someone met it for the first time, there were lots of gifts that were thought appropriate, such as an egg, salt, bread, and sometimes money. It was sometimes said that the baby would never suffer from want if it were given food and money.

By the late twentieth century, the custom was to give money alone. It was usually given straight to the baby, rather than the parent, to maintain the symbolism. In many places, it was believed that you could foretell the baby's future by whether or not it grasped the coin. If it did, it would look after his or her money when it grew up. If it didn't, the child would spend money as fast as it was earned. Even without the coin, if a baby kept its hands mostly closed, it was said it would be good with money.

Seventh Sons

Seventh sons—particularly the seventh son of a seventh son—were once widely believed to have both healing and psychic powers, particularly in Britain, Ireland, France, and Germany. They were also rumored to have a strange power over worms. People released the powers of seventh sons by putting worms into their hands when they were infants and binding the hands until the worms were dead. After this occurred, the seventh son could kill a bucket of worms just by putting his hand in it. And if he were to draw a mark on the ground, any approaching worm would shy away from it as though terrified. If the poor creature actually crossed the line, it would surely and instantly die.

In Ireland, a child born on Whit Sunday, or Pentecost (the seventh Sunday after Easter), was very unfortunate. It was thought that it would either kill or be killed. The only way around the problem was to hold a mock burial—digging a sort of temporary grave and sometimes even constructing a mock coffin out of basketwork or another material that would allow the baby to breathe. The mock coffin would be lowered into the grave, and soil or a piece of turf was placed on top. Once this was done, the baby could be safely removed and future doom was averted.

Naming Names

If you are a superstitious person, you are likely to put a lot of thought into your child's name. It's not a good idea to name a baby after someone you know who has died; if you do, make sure you pick a person who lived a long life—by association, the baby will have one, too.

In Korea and other parts of Asia, no one praises a new baby, to avoid making the evil spirits jealous. Instead, the baby will be given any number of humiliating nicknames.

It is unlucky to turn the bed for a month after a child is born in it.

Looks and Luck

Some people believe that a baby's facial appearance may have a bearing on its future life, and many of these superstitions span cultures right around the world. For example, a baby with large ears will be generous, while one with small ears will be stingy. For the Chinese, a baby born with thick ears or an "inny" belly button is assured of happiness and success. A baby with a large mouth might be a singer or a great speaker, while one with a small mouth will be mean.

Telltale Signs

Marks

In the past, birthmarks and other unusual physical attributes were explained by influences on the mother while she was pregnant. It was believed that strong emotions such as fear, or just the sight of something ugly or out of the ordinary, could mark or shape the baby in some way. In the case of birthmarks, they often appeared in the shape of something the mother was said to have seen. Some people believed that licking the birthmarks as soon as possible after the birth and continuing to do so for some time afterward could cure or remove the mark.

Supposedly, meeting a live hare while she was pregnant could cause a mother to have a baby with a harelip (cleft palate). However, this was not inevitable. If the woman tore her dress or skirt three times, she could prevent the consequences. Just meeting someone carrying a dead hare, however, could cause her to give birth to a baby with a harelip, unless the person had already removed its tail.

Eclipse Warning

In India, there is a belief that a pregnant woman should not go outside during an eclipse or else her baby will be born blind or with a birthmark or scar on its face. On the other side of the globe, in Mayan culture, eclipses were also viewed with suspicion. It was believed that, if a pregnant woman witnessed an eclipse, she would have a baby with a harelip.

Feet First

In Scotland, babies born feet-first were once thought to cure sprains, rheumatism, and lumbago by rubbing the affected part or trampling on it. Another superstition, however, says that a baby born feet-first will grow up to be lame or possibly become lame in an accident. The cure was to rub the baby's

Who to the north, or south, doth set his bed, male children shall beget.

—Robert Herrick, *Hesperides*, 1648

Going Up in the World

In England from the mid-nineteenth century to well into the twentieth century, there was a superstition that newborn babies should always be carried upstairs before they were brought downstairs for the first time.

Midwives were almost always urged to carry the babies upward as a symbolic act, relating to the babies' "going up in the world" later in life. In many cases, new mothers would have given birth on the topmost floor of the house, which made going upstairs something of a challenge. A clever midwife, however, could always find a way around the problem. Babies were often carried up in the midwife's arms while she climbed a ladder or stood on a chair or another piece of furniture, so that she could fulfill the ritual of ensuring her child a better future.

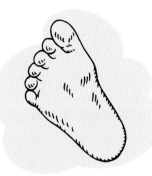

legs with bay leaves. But you had to be able to gather the leaves quickly because this would work only if it was done in the first few hours of the baby's life.

Some superstitions linked to feet include:

- A baby born with webbed toes will never drown and will be generally lucky in life.
- If a male baby's second toe is longer than the first, he will treat his wife badly. If this occurs in a girl, she will dominate the household.
- If the second and third toes are close together, the person will be wealthy.
- A baby born with an extra toe or finger will be lucky.

Nails and Hair

Some people believed that it was very unlucky to cut a baby's nails or hair until it was a year old; otherwise it would make the baby light-fingered (likely to become a thief). It was, however, acceptable to bite the baby's nails instead.

Babies born in May were said to be unlucky. Even worse, a child born on May Day would be afflicted with the evil eye.

Tooth Telling

A baby's teeth can carry a significant number of meanings for both the mother and the baby. A baby born with teeth, or one who teethes early, can mean the mother will soon become pregnant again. Being born with teeth also foretells that the child will:

- have a violent temper
- die a violent death
- be a murderer

- be a vampire
- be extremely clever

If a child's first tooth appeared in its upper jaw, the child would be unlucky or it may not live long. In German superstition, the moment a mother spotted a baby's first tooth, she would slap the baby's face to help it teethe more easily. And a gap between the front teeth bodes well for a baby because it means it will grow up to marry someone wealthy.

Romany gypsies tied a red ribbon around a baby's wrist to protect the baby from curses and spells that would make it ugly.

Dental Digest

The process of getting rid of lost teeth has an array of customs worldwide. In Britain, baby teeth were usually burned with salt sprinkled on them—salt being considered a purifying substance—could keep evil at bay. The earliest reference to this custom goes back to 1686, but it probably originated earlier. It was considered generally unlucky to not burn teeth, but sometimes more specific outcomes were predicted. For example, if a tooth was not burned and an animal found it, the replacement tooth would grow like the animal's tooth. Or if a witch, or anyone with wicked intentions, found the tooth, they may gain power over the person. In some places, people safely preserved their teeth in containers their entire life, and were buried with them. Mothers would sometimes save their children's baby teeth, most likely as part of an older tradition where it was important that a body was buried complete.

In some places, girls would save their teeth for such time as they would have their own children. As mothers, they would hang their teeth around their children's necks to help with teething. Some people chose to make necklaces with animals'

teeth, woodlice, or donkey's hair. Or the teeth and gums could be rubbed with certain types of plants or the mother's wedding ring. These days, we are lucky to have the tooth fairy, a benevolent being that not only takes our teeth and disposes of them safely, but also pays us money for the privilege.

Placing a coral necklace around a baby's neck was thought to help with teething problems. It was also believed to keep babies and children safe from witchcraft and the evil eye.

See Here

In some locations, it was considered unlucky for a baby to see its reflection in a mirror. This precaution was thought to apply until the baby was a certain age (approximately two months to four years old) or until it could talk, or walk, or had teeth. The bad luck that could befall the baby varied, too, including getting rickets, having teething trouble, or becoming cross-eyed. It was also often believed that babies under a year old should not be photographed.

In Jewish tradition, putting candy or other sweets under a new mother's bed keeps evil spirits busy and the baby safe from harm.

Health and Safety

- In Wales, a piece of bread would be hung in a bag around a baby's neck to keep the fairies away.
- In some places in Britain, small pebbles with natural holes in them were hung around children's necks to keep witches away. These were known as "witch stones," "fairy stones," and "eye stones"; in Dorset, they were called "hag stones" or "holy stones." Larger stones with holes were used to cure children of diseases; the child would crawl or be passed through them a number of times. Likewise, sometimes children were passed through brambles or a split ash tree.

Off to a Good Start

**After the baby is born, the mother must take certain
precautions in the first six weeks. Otherwise,
according to superstition, the following can happen:**

- Soon after childbirth, the devil or evil
  spirits have increased power over a woman;
  she should never be left alone, and must
  certainly never go to sleep unless someone else is
  there to watch the child. Otherwise fairies may
  come and swap the child for one of their own.
  Laying a pair of men's pants over the cradle may help prevent
  this from happening.

- During this time, if the mother sticks pins or needles into a curtain, her child
  will have bad teeth.

- The mother cannot walk barefoot. If she does, her child will have a dangerous fall
  when it learns to walk.

- To avoid overall bad luck, a new mother should not give away salt or bread for the
  first six weeks.

- The mother must not enter a stranger's house unless she has
  stopped to buy something in another village first, or
  she will bring ill luck into the home.

A new mother is not
allowed to draw water from
a well, or it will dry up for
seven years.

In Somalia, a garlic amulet worn by both mother and baby for 40 days after the birth will keep evil spirits away.

- In Malaysia, the baby's face would be painted black, with a cross on the forehead and a spot on the nose, so that demons would not recognize the baby and be kept away. Similar face-painting superstitions can be found in India and parts of Africa.
- In China, a black bracelet, talisman, or image of Buddha was used to keep a baby safe and well.
- In Scandinavia, hanging a horsehoe in the nursery was believed to protect the baby against nightmares.
- In a much more specific superstition, in the Dominican Republic, some people believe that hanging a baseball glove over a baby boy's cradle will mean that he will grow up to be a great baseball player.

In the Western Isles of Scotland, it was believed that if you kept the fairies warm at night, your baby would come to no harm.

Cradles, Cribs, and Coffins

- A cradle or stroller must be paid for before a baby sleeps in it, or the baby will die without the means to pay for its coffin.
- It was considered unlucky to buy a new cradle for your first child—some people even believed that the baby would die in this case, too. Therefore, friends or relatives would often purchase it. If you do buy a new cradle, you could pay for it, but don't bring it home until you've had the baby, to avoid tempting fate.

In Jewish tradition, a red thread tied to the cradle or the baby's underwear kept it safe from the evil eye; garlic could also be used.

- If you rock an empty cradle or push an empty stroller, it generally means that a new baby will soon fill it. Although, for some people, it means the baby who uses it will be sick or die. The rule: Think before setting anything in motion.
- A knife placed in the cradle, underneath the mattress, was believed to protect the baby from evil influences. It is very likely that this superstition comes from the belief that iron was resistant to fairies and other supernatural creatures.

For general good health, some superstitions dictate that you place the baby outside in the first April shower after its birth (this obviously has its roots in the Northern Hemisphere) or put a rabbit's foot in the baby's crib. You can also hang a bag of sulfur around the baby's neck or put sulfur in its shoes. Speaking of shoes, one superstition says that having a baby drink boiled water out of a shoe will prevent colic.

Babies born on Halloween have natural protection against evil spirits.

Birthday Cakes

The widespread tradition of a child having a birthday cake with one candle on top for every year of its age is quite a recent one, possibly originating in Germany. Most people believe the child should try and blow the candles out in one breath, if he or she can do so, and make a wish. In Germany traditionally there was one larger candle, called the *Lebenslicht* (light of life), in the middle of the cake, and this was the flame to make a wish on.

Success
& Wealth

For as long as anyone can remember, people have looked for omens or carried tokens to bring good luck, strong health, or increased wealth. Many hunters tend to carry good-luck charms and follow special rituals both before setting off and during the hunt. Sportsmen and women—amateur and professional—also superstitiously perform or say something special or must wear a particular something every time they compete, to help avert back luck. Some are so superstitious they believe they will not be able able to perform properly unless they wear their special shoes or carry out their special preparation rituals. Their unease at not being able to do so can turn this belief into a self-fulfilling prophecy. And fans and spectators can be just as bad as the athletes.

A Prosperous Life

Hunters and sportspeople aren't alone in their superstitious ways. Actors, actresses, and almost everybody associated with live performances have their own ways of calling upon Lady Luck. Even some canny businessmen can't help calling on unseen spirits and forces to bring good luck.

Perhaps the best advice, common in many countries, is not to tempt Fate by speaking about success and wealth before it happens, but to wait until you are certain of it.

Of course, there's much more to good fortune than finding a four-leaf clover or a pot of gold at the end of a rainbow. But, remember, always have enough salt in the house—otherwise, it's out of salt, out of gold.

A-Hunting We Will Go...

When Borneo's Dayak people go hunting, family members who stay at home are forbidden to touch oil or water; if they do, the prey might slip through the hunters' hands.

The children of ancient China's Gilyak hunters were forbidden to draw pictures in sand because it was feared that the lines of the drawings could affect the paths in the forest where their fathers were hunting. If the drawn lines crossed each other, the paths in the forest would do the same, and the hunters would lose their way home.

In Japan, putting a piece of snakeskin in your wallet or purse will bring you riches.

Sympathy Cures

It is a long-held belief that there is a magical or sympathetic link between a wound and the weapon that caused it.

Some of these superstitions include:

- Melanesian hunters who were shot by an arrow believed that if they found the bow that had inflicted the wound, then stored it in the coolest place they could find, it would cool the wound and reduce the swelling. If the assailant kept the bow and put it in a hot place, however, this would worsen the effect of the wound.
- Beginning in the sixteenth century, in England and English-speaking countries, it was believed that, if you kept an object that had inflicted a wound clean and rust-free, it would stop the wound from festering. The superstition of greasing the offending object to be sure it stayed pristine was observed as late as the twentieth century.
- In some places, the wounding weapon was applied to the wound with an ointment or antiseptic to help it heal.

Going Cuckoo

Cuckoos, which are common in Europe, have their fair share of meaning to the superstitious.

- If the call of the first cuckoo of spring comes from your right, you will be prosperous.

- If it comes from your left, the year will be financially unlucky.

- To be certain of prosperity, you had to have money in your pocket when you heard the cuckoo's call. Many people also believed that you had to turn over the money, shake it, jangle it, or spit on it.

- The Welsh believed that the greatest good luck came from trapping a cuckoo, then setting the bird free unharmed.

Good Fortune in Full Flower

Hearing the spring's first cuckoo was not the only "first" considered important to the coming year's success. If you make a wish when you see the first robin of spring, that wish will be granted. After seeing their first robin, most people were on the lookout for the first flowers of spring. Some people believed that the day of the week that you spot your first blooms of the season foretold short- and long-term success in many things.

Monday: You'll have general good fortune.

Tuesday: Your greatest attempts will reap the greatest success.

Wednesday: Your marriage is in trouble.

Thursday: Expect only a meager profit for a while.

Friday: Wealth is on its way.

Saturday: Expect general misfortune.

Sunday: You'll have very good luck in all things for several weeks.

Dreaming of fish swimming in clear water means wealth and power to come.

Cats as Cats Can

Cats are independent and exceptionally enigmatic creatures. So it's no wonder they are closely associated with superstition and suspicion. But not all of those associations are to do with bad luck. Some cat-related beliefs are supposed to foretell future money and success, including:

- A sneezing cat is a sign of future wealth.
- Finding a white hair on a black cat will bring not only wealth, but also happiness.
- Dreaming of an orange cat means you will have luck in money or business.
- In Scotland, an unfamiliar black cat sitting on your porch or doorstep forecasts prosperity.

- In France, some people believed that if they took a black cat to the meeting point of five roads, the cat would lead them to buried treasure.

Many theaters kept a cat to catch vermin and to bring luck. If the cat was seen on a play's opening night, it predicted a good run for the show. If the cat crossed the stage, however, it was considered major bad luck.

Porcelain models of the Japanese beckoning cat, the Maneki Neko, are commonly seen in Asian restaurants and stores. The cat's body language holds significant meaning:

- If the cat is holding its left paw high, it is drawing in customers.
- If the right paw is the high one, it attracts money.

Around the Mediterranean it is said that dreaming of catching a fish means success in the near future.

Bodily Signals

Of course, you might live in a tropical climate with absolutely no cuckoos in sight, or you might be allergic to cats. Then where would you be? Fortunately—or unfortunately—your body is with you wherever you go, and there were all sorts of superstitions related to bodily form and bodily parts that you could draw on to tell your future, should you be so inclined:

- A mole under your left arm meant you would become rich.
- A mole on the back of the neck foretold that you would be beautiful.
- An itchy right palm predicted that money would soon be coming your way.

- An itchy left palm, on the other hand, was an omen that you would be losing money.
- If your right eye twitched, it was a sign of good luck; a twitch in the left eye foretold just the opposite.

Someone with a large gap between their front teeth was believed to possess all-around good luck. Some predictions associated with a gap-toothed grin include:

- wealth and success
- travel to faraway places
- being attractive to the opposite sex

Never hang a new calendar before the New Year begins or you will have bad luck.

Money Matters

Finders Keepers

From as early as the sixteenth century and into the twentieth century, finding money was believed to be unlucky. It had to be spent immediately—ideally on something trivial or a luxury. This was probably a ruse to avoid paying back to someone who claimed they had lost it. Now, that *would* be bad luck.

In England, a sixpence was especially unlucky to find, and many people would leave one where it had fallen. Where money was involved, however, there were usually ways of getting around the bad luck. Some methods included:

- If the coin was crooked or damaged, it was lucky and could be worn as a protective amulet.
- Coins that were bent or had holes, usually sixpences, were often carried or given to others as gifts.

Now and then, it was good luck to find a coin, especially if:

- the coin was heads up
- you had already stepped on it
- you allowed a friend to pick it up on your behalf
- you spat on the coin, reversing the bad luck

Picking up a crown or five-shilling piece had its set of rules and rituals. If these steps weren't followed, the consequences could be:

- general bad luck
- the loss of your job
- bad luck to a member of the cast if you worked in a theater

When playing craps, always blow on the dice before rolling to seal in the good luck.

In the United States, the unluckiest money is a two-dollar bill. But no one agrees on why. Some reasons put forward are its past association with loose morals or dishonesty because a two-dollar bill was:

- the standard price for time with a prostitute in the 1930s
- the price of a vote in rigged elections, in the days when election rigging and vote buying were the norm, and two dollars could be the amount of a day's wages
- a standard bet in horse racing: Bookmakers would pay out in two-dollar notes. Having a wad of two-dollar bills marked you as a gambler at a time when betting on the ponies was prohibited and seen as an indication of low character.

Sometimes the devil is blamed for the unluckiness of these notes because the word "deuce" is a slang name for him. Some superstitious Americans counter the bad luck of a two-dollar

Handselling

"Handselling" is the belief that the first money a tradesman, stallholder, or storekeeper takes is lucky, and means good luck for the rest of the day. Many people would spit on their first money of the day to increase their luck. But the pressure to get that important handsel (or hansel, from the Middle English *hansel*) could mean accepting any offer, however small, for the first sale. This left sellers open to exploitation by people making an unreasonable offer. Even so, many people would sell for below cost just to get the handsel and to start the day's business.

bill by tearing off one corner. When all four corners are gone, the note is discarded.

> In Trinidad and Tobago, it is believed that if you put your handbag on the floor, you will never have money.

Carrying a Coin for Good Luck

In the United Kingdom, old coins had an image of a cross on them, to keep away the devil. It was believed that an empty purse or wallet gave the devil carte blanche and influence over the unprotected owner.

> *The deuille may daunce in crossless purse when coyne hathe tooke his tyde*
>
> Thomas Drant, *Horace*, 1566

A related superstition is putting money—usually a coin—into a purse or handbag when it is given as a gift, to protect the recipient from the devil.

Buying and Selling

Over the centuries of humans' wheeling and dealing, for both vendors and purchasers every transaction was fraught with the possibility of good or bad luck. Even the people or animals a seller or trader met on the way to the market could be construed as an omen. It was bad luck for your business if you crossed paths with:

- hares
- single magpies
- crows

Dreaming of cooking or eating fish means that there will be a happy ending for a current project.

But you would smile at your good fortune if you saw:

- black cats (but not for everyone)
- fair-haired people
- five magpies for silver
- six magpies for gold

Even in today's world of financial trading, superstitions are common. Some traders wear only the tie they wore on a particularly successful day, while some have lucky socks (hopefully, regularly washed). Others perform lucky rituals before work each day or before making important telephone calls. It seems that stratospheric incomes can't help to insulate these dealmakers from their fear of the unknown.

There is even a superstition that the result of gridiron football's Super Bowl will let traders know whether to look forward to a bull or a bear stock market over the following year. A win for a team from the American Football Conference

(AFC) foretells that the market will be down. If a team from the National Football Conference (NFC) wins, the stock market for the coming year will be bullish.

Backhanders

Luck money or a luck penny is a term used for a small proportion of the purchase price in a transaction that is returned to the buyer in order to secure the future success of

Suit Yourself

New clothes are the subject of many superstitions, and most involve adding money to the clothes for good luck. These traditions began in the middle of the nineteenth century, and are still common today.

In Britain, it was typical for a tailor to put a halfpenny in each pocket of a man's new suit. Some put an additional halfpenny in each subsequent pocket, so the second received a whole penny, and so on. This superstition was supposed to ensure that the suit's owner would always have money.

In another well-dressed tradition, a young boy wearing a new suit for the first time would visit each of his neighbors, and they would give him coins for his pockets. Some people believed that it was important to put the money into the right pocket. If it went into the left pocket, the person who placed it there would always want for money.

Other clothing superstitions include:

- Never iron a shirt tail, or you will iron the money out of it.
- If you find two pins placed in a cross under your lapel, you will get the best of the day's bargains.
- If you mend your clothes while wearing them, you will never grow rich.

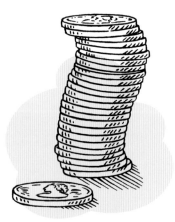

both parties. It could also symbolize that neither person wished bad luck on the item bought and sold, particularly if a deal involved live animals. It could also have worked as a commission fee, especially if the deal was done on behalf of a third party. Luck money was exchanged well into the twentieth century. Some similar superstitions include:

- "God's penny" was money exchanged to bind two parties to a future transaction.
- Earnest money was given to a servant when hired, as a symbol that both employer and employee would stick to the agreement made about the duties, rates of pay, time off, and other details.

In China, one of the many New Year superstitions is to give children a lucky red envelope containing money. This symbolically wishes them wealth and success in the year ahead.

Taking the Bait

Fishermen and their families have many superstitions, which is not surprising because the job involves so much danger and unpredictability. Certain words were believed to cause bad luck and were avoided when mending nets or preparing for the next fishing trip, and while on the trip itself—all in the name of not tempting Fate. Some words to skip included:

- church
- minister
- salmon
- egg
- cat
- pig
- rabbit
- hare
- rat

Bee Very Aware

It is a long-held belief that bees are attuned to the human world. Some people feel that they are quick to take offense. Therefore, a collection of superstitions arose that are mindful of bees, including:

- Selling a hive of bees was frowned upon in rural communities from the eighteenth to the twentieth century. Paying for the hive in gold, however, could allay any possible adversity in the future.
- It wasn't good luck to give your bees away, but they could be bartered. In Devon, England, the usual payment was a small pig or a sack of corn.
- If a bee lands on your hand, it means that money will be coming to you in the future; if it lands on your head, you are destined for greatness.

Grate Expectations

The fear of sympathetic magic—a belief that something affecting one object will also impact related objects—is often at the root of many superstitions. Therefore, some farmers believed that:

- If you burned milk, your cows would slow or stop milk production.
- If you threw eggshells onto a fire, your chickens would stop laying eggs.

At the hearth, cinders thrown from a fire were used to predict the future. A round cinder represented a purse; the lucky person it flew toward would come into money. Other shapes also foretold wealth, but only if the cinder clinked like the sound of coins.

Dreaming of catching a fish means success in the near future. The bigger the fish, the bigger the success.

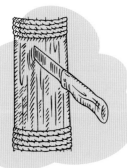

Fishing for Luck

Many fishing superstitions were attempts to ward off bad luck; however, there were some rituals to attract good luck. Some sailors stuck a knife into the mast of a fishing vessel to have a good voyage. If the wind should fail, the same action could bring the wind back. There was also a widespread belief that throwing a small coin into the sea bought you a good wind.

Superstitious fishermen—and that was most of them— would not sail or start anything new, such as changing from line fishing to lobster-pot fishing, on a Friday. Saturday, Sunday, and Monday were good days for new beginnings or tasks.

On the Isle of Man, off England's west coast, any money that was left over after distributing the profits from a fishing trip was given to the poor. The fishermen believed their luck would improve if they remembered the less fortunate.

Many fishermen threw back the first fish they caught, believing many more would come to replace it.

Tips with Tea

In times past, many people believed that there was much more to tea than reading the leaves to predict the future:

- Throwing away used tea leaves would encourage poverty.

- Burning tea on the fire would bring wealth.

- Bubbles in your tea meant money would be coming.

The fishermen of St. Malo, France, have an interesting ritual of their own. At the start of each new season, they pour wine down the throat of the first fish they catch, then throw it back. They hope the other fish will see the drunken fish, and rush to join the party.

In many fishing communities, it is considered bad luck to count the number of fish you have caught before the end of the day. If you are foolish enough to do so, you've counted your final catch for the day.

Dream of an empty fishing net and it means that bad luck is on the way.

Exam Success

Success isn't always measured in terms of money. Students all over the world have rituals they perform before and on examination days. Some use new pencils because they have never written an incorrect answer and, hopefully, won't do so now. Others opt for the pencil or pen they used while they were studying, hoping it will remember the correct answers.

In Poland, it is a popular ritual to kick other people's legs on the way into the exam room, and to blow on your fingers, which seems to be a multinational tradition. Russian students won't make their bed, cut their fingernails, or wear anything new.

You were very fortunate if small black spiders landed on you, because this was supposed to foretell money.

Money Spinner

By the late sixteenth century, spiders in your house were thought to bring good luck. Other good-luck superstitions

included putting the spider in your pocket, eating it—not so lucky for the spider—or whirling it round your head three times. These well recorded rituals could explain why a spider was sometimes called a "spinner," and the origins of the terms "money spinner" and "money spider." Of course, a more prosaic explanation is that spiders spin webs.

Performing Rites

Stage Frights

The theatrical world has a long and very rich history of superstitious tradition—both on and off the stage. The most famous superstition is to never wish a performer good luck,

The Scottish Play

One of the most entrenched superstitions is that it's very bad luck to mention Shakespeare's *Macbeth* in a theater. Some people won't mention it anywhere and refer to it only as the "Scottish play."

This superstition may have developed because:

- The play's hazardous sword fights injured many actors, some seriously, during these scenes.

- The three witches and their spells may have frightened early audiences.

- There is so much darkness and destruction in the story.

- *Macbeth* is associated with failing theaters: Playhouses with low ticket sales would put it on to attract more crowds.

but instead to say "Break a leg!" This could be another way to avoid tempting Fate, but there are other explanations:

- A stage curtain is also called a "leg," and a successful, long run would mean many curtain calls, causing the machinery that raises and lowers the curtain to break or wear out.
- The saying could also refer to a bow, where the leg of the actor is "broken," or bent. It is therefore hoped that the actor performs so well, he'll need to take many bows.
- Some people believe it refers to the indomitable French actress Sarah Bernhardt (1844–1923), whose career continued after her leg was amputated.
- Other people believe it began when John Wilkes Booth, the actor who assassinated U.S. President Abraham Lincoln, broke a leg jumping from the President's box onto the stage. It's difficult, however, to see the good luck in that story.

In the world of the stage, a good dress rehearsal means a bad opening performance and perhaps a shorter run than expected.

Stage No-nos

Other theatrical bad-luck omens include whistling or clapping while backstage. There is, however, a logical origin for these beliefs. Before electricity controlled suspended or "flying" scenery and props, the cues for moving them were whistles and claps. If a whistle or clap was heard at the wrong time, a heavy piece of scenery could seriously hurt an actor or damage a stage prop.

Offstage Outrages

Some stage superstitions could cause offence to members of the audience—perhaps this is why they have persisted.

Some examples include:

- A front-of-house manager will often insist a paying patron be admitted before anyone with a complimentary ticket.

- On the 1866 New York opening night of *The Black Crook*, perhaps the first American musical, the house manager refused to let a woman into the theater first, on the grounds this would ruin the success of the play. He later claimed the show's successful run of 474 performances was directly due to his care.

If an actor is met at the door by the theatre's house cat, he counts himself very lucky, and believes the show will be a great success.

Games of Chance

Some of the toughest sportsmen and women are known to be superstitious, and each sport seems to have its own mascots, beliefs, and fears. Most teams have mascots, and many players carry charms or wear particular clothes for luck. To encourage good luck, some superstitious baseball players will spit into their hand before they pick up the bat. Others stick chewing gum on their caps before a game or make sure that they step on one of the bases before leaving the field after an inning.

Also in baseball, when a pitcher is throwing a perfect game or a no-hitter, no one says anything about it to him or it may ruin the streak. The same applies to a shut-out in professional ice hockey—no one mentions it to the goalie during the game.

Lucky Sportspeople

In soccer, a double number on a player's shirt is supposed to be lucky. Some players have other superstitious rituals related to their outfit, such as tying their bootlaces in an intricate kind of knot—every time.

Golfers will often only begin a game with odd-numbered clubs, and some carry coins in their pockets for good fortune. Ice hockey players may tap the goalie's shin pads before a game, and always put their pads and skates on in the same order.

In the NHL, some hockey players refuse to shave during the Stanley Cup playoffs, leading to the infamous playoff beard. Tennis players avoid stepping on the lines on the court before a match, and walk around the outside of the court when swapping sides.

In 10-pin bowling, the perfect score is 300, so some players include the number on their car license plate for good luck.

Star Stories
Many famous athletes tend to have interesting rituals of their own, including:

- Basketball player Michael Jordan graduated from the University of North Carolina, and superstitiously always wore U.N.C. shorts under his Chicago Bulls uniform for good luck. To cover them, he had to wear longer shorts. Soon afterward, the standard length of NBA shorts was changed.
- Major League pitcher Turk Wendell always brushed his teeth and chewed black licorice between each inning.
- Mark "The Bird" Fidrych, of Detroit Tigers fame, talked to himself and to the ball before pitching.
- Major League baseball player Wade Boggs ate only chicken on the day of a game, and drew a special symbol meaning "to life" in the ground before each turn to bat.
- Hockey legend Wayne Gretzky never cut his hair when on the road because, when he did once, his team lost.

Spirits
& Souls

Over the centuries, the spirits and souls of the dead have been respected and feared by many people from many cultures. A variety of superstitions and burial traditions developed to keep the spirits of the dead happy, and therefore prevent them from returning and haunting people on Earth. To satisfy the spirits, practical and beautiful objects were placed in the tomb. In ancient Egypt, these were wrapped in the layers of a mummy's cotton bindings. In some cultures, it was the living who needed to be protected from the dead—particularly if their souls were not happy—and equally elaborate rituals and superstitions grew up surrounding the need to keep the living from possible harm.

Restless Spirits

Today, annual festivals celebrate dying as an important part of the human life cycle. During these celebrations—such as Día de Los Muertos, or the Day of the Dead, in Mexico—it is common to honor ancestor spirits by wearing symbolic masks and costumes that are meant to protect the living.

Blood and Bone

Most early cultures believed in a soul that could exist separately. Some people thought that bones, especially those of the skull, were the home of the soul or life spirit. They were therefore often used for magic rituals and medicines.

- Northern Europeans made vessels out of their enemies' skulls and drank from them, hoping to gain some of the dead person's strength or spirit.
- Some people spit for good luck because blood and spittle were also thought to be the dwelling place of the soul.
- It was believed by some that a murdered man's soul could recognize and accuse the murderer of the crime because the victim's blood, as the physical and earthly home of the soul, would gush out of its dead body to accuse its slayer.

A sudden silence when people are talking means that a soul was present and passed by.

Bee Cautious

Some cultures believe that the spirit or soul becomes separated from the body during sleep. This belief is echoed in the Buddhist philosophical text *Brihadaranyaka Upanishad*, which says it is unwise to wake someone suddenly because the

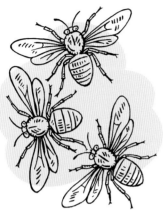

spirit might not have enough time to return. This superstition can be found in many international folk stories, and it is often associated with bees. The idea of a bee soul is part of the following tale from the Scottish Highlands:

Two nineteenth-century travelers lay down to rest and one fell asleep. The other noticed a bee go into a small hole, and he trapped it with the end of his staff. When he tried to wake his companion, he found he couldn't. But once he removed his stick from the hole, the bee flew out and into the ear of the sleeping man, who then woke up.

When he asked about the sleeper's dreams, the man replied: "I dreamt that you had shut me up in a dark cave, and I could not awake until you let me out."

A buzzing in your ear means that a soul in purgatory is calling for a prayer.

Naturally, the man concluded that the sleeper's soul was in the bee. And it was a common superstition to believe the sleeper would not awaken, or would die, if the bee were not returned to his ear. In another version from Scotland, the person did wake but became insane:

A young lad was sleeping outside on a sunny slope, when somebody came upon him and roughly wakened him. The lad was practically insane thereafter, but a skilled person was consulted. He said that the lad should go back to sleep where he was the year before, then be allowed to wake up of his own accord. As the boy slept, the wondering onlookers saw a beautiful bee come along and enter the lad's mouth. When he awoke, he was perfectly sane and sound.

Spirited Birds

Birds hold an important place in the spiritual world. Human spirits that cannot find rest are said to haunt the Earth as lapwings, sparrows, or swifts. Seagulls and other seabirds are thought to be the souls of fishermen or mariners lost at sea. Therefore, some superstitious sailors will not feed a seagull or look one in the eye when swimming or clinging to a wreck, in case the gull picks out their eyes and leaves them to die. Even worse, a seagull flying in a long, straight line is said to be a soul following its corpse on the sea floor. The bird will not rest until the body is buried.

Petting Precautions

Superstitions abound about cats and dogs, perhaps because their lives are so intertwined with our own. For a long period of time, there was a popular belief that cats and dogs could see ghosts or the spirits of the dead. It was thought:

- If a dog howled at night or scratched holes in the ground as though digging a grave, it was anticipating a death.
- If a dog or cat jumped over a body, it was bad luck for its spirit, and therefore the animal had to be killed to reverse the effect. Some superstitious households removed their family pets immediately following a death at home.
- Buddhists belived that cats were the temporary resting places of extremely spiritual people.
- Cats are capable of astral travel, and possess the power of hypnotism.
- Druids felt that cats were humans who were being punished for evil acts during their lives.
- A cat on top of a tombstone signaled that the soul of the body buried beneath was possessed by the devil.
- In Japan, it was believed that spirits of the dead sometimes take the form of female cats.

A child born at midnight, known as a chime child, can see souls and spirits at will.

Trading Places

Looking down to see your body—often at the point of going to sleep or in near-death experiences—is often explained as the spirit looking at the body. This type of experience can lead to a spirit traveling to different places and meeting other people, and is usually described as "astral travel." A separated spirit, which appears only while that person is alive, is a person's spectral double. This spirit, sometimes called a "wraith," may be:

- summoned in love divinations to see a future spouse or lover
- seen in a ritual called "porch watching," where a person sitting on a church porch at midnight, often on Halloween, is thought to be able to see all the people in the parish who will die during the next year
- seen just before the moment of death; it is not uncommon for people to report seeing a vision of someone, then to learn the person had died at the same moment somewhere far away.

One-Way Traffic

There is an old European superstition that anyone who gave a cow to the poor during his lifetime would be rewarded after death by the cow guiding him along the perilous "soul road" to heaven. Another myth says that the Milky Way is the soul road, so the connection between the name and cows may not be a coincidence. Bridges were also thought to be used as soul roads. And rainbows were believed to be another path to heaven, especially for the souls of children, who would be guided across it by their guardian angels.

Star Signs

Are stars human souls? They are, according to pagan myths. In Britain, a falling star foretold a birth. The star being the soul of the new baby coming to Earth to join its body. In other countries, a falling star meant that a soul had been released from purgatory to continue its journey to heaven.

Soul Searching

There are many superstitions about where souls go. Some people believed that they resided in flowers as such thyme or foxglove. More often, souls were thought to rest in animals and insects. It's unsurprising that there are many superstitions involving butterflies because of their graceful beauty:

- Butterflies were often believed to be the souls of the dead.
- Children were warned not to harm a butterfly because it could be the soul of a dead loved one.

The seventh son of a seventh son has the gift of healing and the ability to see spirits.

- Some Christians thought that the soul was a butterfly that hovered over Earth while waiting to enter purgatory.
- Ancient Egyptians believed that the soul left the body the way a butterfly leaves a chrysalis.
- In Burma, the *win-laik-pya*, or soul butterfly, is said to leave the body when it sleeps and meet up with the soul butterflies of other people and animals. The superstitious will also not wake a sleeping person suddenly in case the soul butterfly does not have time to return and the sleeper dies.
- In Gaelic tradition, the newly dead are thought to be visible as a butterfly hovering over the corpse. In Ireland, this is a sign of happiness for the soul.

Going, Going, Gone

If someone was acting erratically, it was often thought that an evil spirit was in possession of their body and soul. Many people turned to exorcism as an answer, and these rituals were performed worldwide. Although it is currently not a widespread practice, some Christian priests still perform these ceremonies.

Running water is often said to keep away evil, especially witches and vampires.

Multichannel Reception

Receiving messages and ideas from the souls of people who died long ago, then writing down music or poetry on their behalf, is called "channeling." The people who acquire the messages are known as mediums, spiritualists, or psychics.

Mediums claim they can contact individual souls of the dead, often with the help of an object the person owned in life, or in the presence of a living relative. Sometimes people who are not superstitions have difficulty explaining the apparent accuracy of messages that appear to be from beyond the grave.

In any case, it is certainly true that mediums in the Western world make a good deal of money from those who consult them. In the rest of the world, witch doctors or shamans, from the jungles of Brazil to the remote mountains of Papua New Guinea, all claim that their power, insight, and forecasts come from contacts in the spirit world.

Devilish Deterrents

Spirit Measures

There are many superstitions about the best way to deter demons, devils, and other supernatural creatures, as well keeping the souls or spirits of the dead at bay. Some ways to stay safe included:

- standing inside a circle
- folding your thumbs inside your other fingers
- crossing your fingers; in the eighteenth century, this was thought to prevent evil spirits from influencing the deceased as well as protect against ghosts.

The Maya people of the Yucatan drew a chalk line from the grave to the hearth of the deceased's home, so the soul could find its way back to visit.

Chinese people traditionally believed that spirits traveled only in straight lines, and were easily confused or distracted. Zigzag bridges were built to stop their passage, and to ensure that the dead were allowed to rest in peace. During Chinese funeral processions, people often threw fake money along the route or banged on gongs to distract any demons.

Ancient Babylonians who believed they were targeted or troubled by evil spirits placed figures of them in miniature boats and pushed them into open water. The Babylonians hoped the boats would capsize and drown the evil spirits.

Shadowy Beliefs

The belief that a person's shadow was a visible manifestation of the soul was once very common worldwide, and many people still believe that treading on someone's shadow brings him or her

Mirror Images

A living person's reflection is generally thought to be a likeness of their soul, or contain a strong link to it. Around the world, some superstitious people still believe that their picture is so closely related to their soul that spells can be wrought by anyone who has their image. While there are people who simply do not like to have their photo taken, there are others who will cover their faces with their hands to protect their souls.

In Africa, the Basuto people believe that a crocodile snapping at a man's reflection in water has the power to seize the reflection and drag it underwater, and so kill the man. The Zulu tradition says that it is dangerous to look into a dark pool because a hidden spirit may seize the reflection and steal your soul.

bad luck. In more recent times, builders would cast someone's shadow on a foundation stone, measure the shadow with a piece of string, and bury the string under the foundation stone. Unfortunately, the person measured was expected to die within 12 months because their soul had been captured, and the Earth spirits were appeased. In another variation, eastern Europeans believed a building would stand safely only if something live was laid in its foundation, as a sacrifice to the Earth spirits.

To draw a spirit to you, write the name of the spirit on parchment, then burn the parchment while repeating sacred words.

Close Those Eyes!

Some people believed that an evil spirit in a body was the reason why a corpse's eyes do not close naturally. It was feared the spirit was looking for the next victim through the open eyes, and another death in the household was imminent.

Body and Soul

There are many superstitions about what to do once the soul has departed:

- Ancient cultures such as the Egyptians buried material goods to be used in the afterlife with the body. The body was also preserved or mummified so it would be prepared to rejoin its spirit at resurrection.
- Important Vikings and ancient rulers in Britain were buried with their treasures under massive manmade mounds. Others were burned at sea in a ship full of their greatest possessions.
- Civilizations as far back as Ur in 2600 B.C. usually entombed slaves, horses, and faithful companions with dead rulers.

In Japan, it is believed there is a spirit in every rock, tree, mountain, river, and grain of sand. It's also believed there is a female spirit in every taxicab and a god of the toilet.

- When Visigoth king Alaric died in A.D. 410, his people diverted a river in Busento, Italy, buried him, and restored the river's old channel. To be sure the burial stayed secret and was not looted, the slaves who diverted the river were also killed and buried there.

Soul Food

In Europe, the recently deceased could relieve their soul of any stress or worry through a ritual called "sin-eating." Bread, beer, and money were passed over the corpse to someone presumably not superstitious or who was particularly hungry—sin-eaters were often beggars. When the sin-eater ate the bread, drank the beer, and took the money, the dead person's sins were transferred, releasing the soul from its burden.

- Some African people make "soul pots" filled with goods the dead person might want from the living world.
- Ashanti men make *abusua kuruwa*, or family pots, where they place all of the hair shaved by the mourning blood relatives.
- In parts of Europe, food for the dead was left at graveyards or crossroads.

Souls and spirits are easier to see and contact at midnight and on the anniversaries of their deaths.

Touch and Go

Superstitions abound to assure that souls of the dead would be laid to rest and not haunted. Some of the traditions include:

- Touching the corpse of someone dear to you was thought the best way to avoid being haunted by him or her. This is from an anonymous account about the notorious early eighteenth-century Scottish pirate John Gow, who plundered ships mostly off the coasts of Portugal and Spain, and his lady friend:

The lady whose affections Gow had engaged, went up to London to see him before his death, and arriving too late had the courage to request a sight of his dead body; and then, touching the hand of the corpse she formally resumed the troth-plight which she had bestowed. Without going through this ceremony, she could not, according to the superstition of the country, have escaped a visit from the ghost of her departed lover, in the event of her bestowing upon any living suitor the faith which she had plighted to the dead.

- An iron cross on a burial site kept the spirit in place.
- Mirrors were turned or covered in case the face of the

departed was seen, which meant that the soul was waiting inside the house for the next inhabitant to die.

- Washing the threshold of the house immediately after the body left prevented the spirit's return.
- In India, a sprig of holy basil was placed in the coffin to ensure the spirit a comfortable journey.
- In England, perishable foods such as butter, milk, meat, and onions were thrown away after a death in the house, in case the soul had corrupted them.
- In Scotland, sticking a nail or another iron object into perishable foodstuffs prevented a spirit invasion. Whisky was also protected from losing its strength and depth.

Open Doors

Just as superstitious people thought the dying sometimes needed help to pass on, so they also thought the soul of the recently departed needed to move on and stay away. To ease the soul's journey, they would open all of the doors and windows, and unlock every lock.

To see resident souls and spirits in a cemetery, medieval spell books recommend burning a mixture of aloe, musk, saffron, vervain, and pepper.

Weather or Not

For some people, the weather could tell you the state of someone's soul:

- Thunder after a funeral signaled that the departed's soul had reached heaven.
- Showers on an open grave meant the soul of the person to be buried was happy.
- A hurricane was a sign that the deceased had committed a sin that had never been discovered, had led a bad life, or had made a pact with the devil.

The Graveyard Shift

In Europe, North America, and other parts of the world, some children held their breath while passing a graveyard in case they would breathe in the soul of someone recently deceased. In Britain and parts of France, the soul or spirit of the last person to be buried watched over a graveyard until the next person took over. They also summoned the next person to die. In another version, the first person in the parish to die each year kept watch for the next 12 months. They rode in a ghostly horsedrawn cart, stopping at the door of the next person to die, and took his or her soul away with them.

If elder planted in the shape of a cross on a new grave bloomed, it meant that the dead person's soul was happy.

Dance Your Cares Away

In Greece, dancing around an enemy's burial site kept the person's spirit from returning for revenge. Perhaps this is why some people relish the idea of dancing on someone's grave. In

Self-Help Hauntings

In nineteenth-century Britain, the bodies of suicides could not be buried in consecrated ground, so they were interred beside the public highway with a wooden stake driven through them. This probably happened to deter others from suicide, rather than to prevent the dead walking. Yet stories are still told about ghosts appearing where suicides were buried because it was believed that the bodies of suicide victims did not decompose until the time they would have died from natural causes.

Candles in the Wind

Faint dancing lights over people who have recently died or over new graves are known as "corpse lights" or "corpse candles." Many superstitious people believe that they signify the soul leaving the body.

Stories of these sightings date back at least to the Icelandic sagas of the early thirteenth century, when the lights were seen over burial mounds and were said to be the souls of warriors guarding their treasure. In other stories, a light is said to travel from a churchyard to the house where someone is about to die. It is believed to be the soul of a relative of the dying person coming to summon him or her.

In fact, toward the end of World War I, mysterious lights were seen along the coast of Cornwall in England. People said that the lights were the souls of Cornish sailors who had returned to protect their homeland after being drowned by German submarine action. They flashed their corpse lights to lure German ships or submarines to destruction. No other ships saw the lights, and all other craft besides those of the Germans passed by safely.

In Malaysia, someone suspected of being possessed is pinched and hit on the head.

Spain, it was traditional to dance seven times around the body to ensure the soul's peace.

Begone!
Some popular rituals to protect your house from malicious and malevolent spirits include:

- Remove a door, then rehang it with the hinges on the other side.
- Hang rowan and Saint-John's-wort over a doorway.
- Draw an unbroken line in chalk across a doorstep.

- Grow violets in or around your house, and ivy on the walls.
- Hang garlic over a door and, whenever a spirit threatens, bite a clove and toss it away from the house—it will take the spirit with it.
- Light bonfires and other bright lights.

Knot Wanted!

Rituals to confine a troublesome ghost, spirit, or soul to its grave include:

- Gather knotgrass under the light of a waning moon. Take it to where the ghost lives, tie one knot in it, and bury it there.
- In Denmark, a simple wooden post driven into the site did the trick. If the post was removed, however, the ghost would be released.
- In Iceland, it is believed that you should tie 7, 14, or 21 knots in a rope, while naming the soul you wish to restrict. Next, bury this outside your home to keep it safe from the spirit, or burn the rope to release the spirit into another existence.

A soul or spirit will most likely appear during New Year's celebrations, festivals such as Halloween, and the Mexican Day of the Dead, which welcomes souls back to Earth with special food and celebrations.

Personal Measures

It was once believed that children born on Christmas Day were free from ever seeing an evil spirit. Anyone born on the other 364 days of the year had to do what they could to protect themselves, such as:

Hush Duppies

In Jamaica, many people believe the soul of a dead person goes to Heaven immediately, but his spirit, or duppy, stays for a while, sometimes permanently. Some people believe that the duppy rises three days after burial, and returns to the house until the ninth night, when it finally leaves. Therefore, a wake or all-night vigil is sometimes held on the ninth night after death. Other beliefs were:

- Placing 10 coffee beans in the room of a dead person prevents a duppy from entering because they can only count up to nine.

- To keep a duppy from returning to haunt others, everyone must say goodbye to the body, and every child must be lifted and passed over the coffin while the name of the deceased is said.

- Tears must fall on the body or else its duppy will haunt the mourner.

- When you leave a wake, you cannot say who is going with you—simply touch them. Otherwise the duppy might follow you home.

- In the Middle Ages, candles were left near beds to drive away spirits.
- On Halloween, turnips with lit candles inside were carried for protection. These were the original jack-o'-lanterns.
- Tying a sprig of rosemary inside a seashell with red thread.
- Angelica and nettle were worn or carried as an amulet.
- Asking a ghost what it wants so it will disappear forever.
- Burning frankincense and myrrh in your home to give spirits peace and rest.

If none of the above worked and a ghost was chasing you, it was suggested that you jump into or cross running water. A spirit couldn't follow you because moving water represented life.

Magical Little People

All around the world, there is a general belief in magical little people who could influence our lives. The tooth fairy—sometimes known as the tooth mouse or tooth rat in England—who exchanges money for children's baby teeth, is benign and well loved. But there are other tiny creatures that some people believe play nasty tricks, wreak havoc, and cause general annoyance. From Peter Pan's Tinkerbell to the "little people" of Ireland and the *kappa*, or water spirits, of Japan, if you are of a mind to believe in wee folk and their powers—supernatural or otherwise—then there is a whole otherworld of folklore, magic, and superstition out there waiting for you to explore.

It's a Small World

*Curiously, there is a common thread of belief
in several different cultures that sprites, fairies,
gnomes, dwarves, and goblins are the descendants
of early inhabitants of an area who were displaced
by bigger, tougher invaders.*

Sprites

In Britain, the term "sprite" covers many legendary and magical beings, such as fairies, elves, and dwarves. Even though the word "sprite" is from the Latin *spiritus*, meaning "spirit," it is rarely used to mean the soul or spirit of the dead.

Descriptions of sprites differ from country to country, but they tend to have similar customs or characteristics. Sprite-related superstitions are usually meant to protect people from the magic and mischiefmaking of sprites believed to dislike humans, or hoping to keep sprites happy.

Purely to cause mischief, elves might tangle your hair into snarled elflocks, or elfin locks, while you sleep—giving you a very bad hair day.

Fairies

Pretty female fairies with long hair and gossamer wings are a relatively recent invention. The modern word "glamour" originally meant the kind of enchantment or magical attraction and power possessed by fairies. Early believers in fairies thought that they resembled themselves, but in some cultures fairies were said to be taller than humans, or able to change in size. But they were always slim and had an ethereal, otherworldly look.

Bottled Sprite

If you wanted to catch a troublesome sprite, the easiest way was to weave red thread to form a net at the top of a forked stick of ash or rowan, and place the sticks at the front and back of a house or building.

A more complex trap required a stick of blackthorn and a copper wire that had never carried electricity. The wire had to be bound to the stick with red thread, then positioned where the sprite had been observed.

A lit candle placed in front of the trap would attract the sprite overnight. In the morning, the trap holding the captured sprite was taken away, and the red thread was cut with a knife and put into a bottle. With the accompaniment of a magic spell, the bottle would be sealed with a cork and red wax, then buried.

Fairy Speculations

All fairies were believed to have magical powers, including the power to fly, but the idea of wings was rarely described before the nineteenth century. Small fairies were thought to fly on stems of ragwort, or on the backs of birds. And there were only two ways to see fairies: by looking through a blade of grass bent into a circle or by calling out their true but secret name.

There have always been conflicting views on the origin of fairies, which were usually said to live underground in hills or burial mounds, at the horizon or across the sea, or even at the bottom of the garden. They have been thought to be:

- the souls of the dead, who inhabit a parallel world to our own, and could be seen only by those with second sight
- angels cast out of heaven, but not sent to hell
- a totally different species—neither angels nor humans
- Stone Age humans driven into hiding by other humans who had developed the ability to use iron. When flint

arrowheads were discovered, they were sometimes called "elf shot." *Elf* and *fairy* were often interchangeable terms.

Fairy Pranks

The pranks fairies played ranged from mild to sinister. Superstitious people believed it was easy to offend fairies, and a good idea to avoid areas they inhabited or frequented. Anyone caught and taken to the land of the fairies was warned to never eat any food while there, or they might not escape.

Fairies lead travelers in wrong directions and send them astray.

Fairy *Feng Shui*

Much like the Eastern belief in *feng shui*, Western cultures once believed in the existence of fairy paths. People avoided building on them; for added protection, they built houses with the front and back entrances aligned. The doors were left open at night so fairies could travel through unimpeded.

How to Keep a Fairy Far Away

Some methods to keep fairies at bay included:

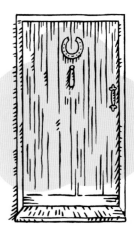

- keeping iron objects in the house, such as an iron horseshoe over the door—this could be linked to the theory of Iron Age invaders overthrowing Stone Age peoples
- building your home near running water
- wearing your clothes inside out
- ringing bells, especially church bells, although fairies on horseback were often said to have bells on the harnesses
- planting Saint-John's-wort or four-leaf clover
- gathering charms made of rowan and herbs for outdoor protection, although in some places rowan trees were believed to be sacred to fairies
- baking bread, because freshly baked bread is a symbol of a happy home and hearth

Fairy Gifts

In Celtic folklore, people often offered bread, cream, and butter to the fairies. But you had to be careful with these gifts or you might get something in return; if Scottish children piled cabbage stalks around the windows and doors of their homes during Halloween, the fairies were likely to bring them a new brother or sister.

Fairies love to steal or hide small objects left lying around the house.

Against the Grain

In Scotland, many people once believed that it was dangerous to go into a mill after dark because this was when fairies brought their grain to be ground, and they did not like to be seen. This superstition could, however, have been started by a clever miller who wanted to prevent theft at night.

Ring Cycles

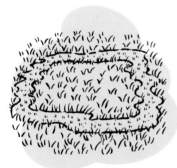

In European superstitious folklore, circles of mushrooms or withered grass on lawns or fields, and in woodland glades, are believed to be rings caused by fairies, elves, or witches. In Britain, they were said to be the result of fairies dancing at night. Other people believed that they grew above an underground fairy settlement. In reality, fairy rings are made when an underground fungus sends threads called *hyphae* outward from a central point. The fungus alters the balance of nutrients in the soil, changing its hue and strength, and the appearance of anything growing on the surface. Mushrooms are the outward growth of the fungus, but they do not become visible until the season and weather are right. Next, the mushrooms spore and start the growth cycle of another ring. There are approximately 60 mushroom species capable of creating these circular patterns. Some of these fairy rings have been grown as large as 900 feet (275 m) in diameter.

There are numerous fairy-ring superstitions, including:

- If you ran around a fairy ring under a full moon, you would hear the fairies talking and laughing below.
- It was very bad luck if you ran around a fairy ring more than nine times—not to mention tiring!
- If you sat inside a fairy ring on Beltane, or May Eve (April 30th), or on Halloween, you could fall under an enchantment or find yourself stolen away to the land of the fairies.
- Cattle and sheep were believed to understand the dangers of fairy rings, so therefore would not graze inside them.
- If you attempted to destroy a ring, the fairies would wreak terrible and magical revenge on you.
- If a ring was dug up or disturbed, it would soon reappear.

Fairies would ride animals at night, making them run to exhaustion.

Know Your Little Folk

Redcaps

A redcap is a particularly nasty British sprite with sharp claws and pointed teeth. Redcaps are rumored to live in ruined castles on the English-Scottish border and murder anyone who entered their home—either by tearing them apart with their claws or crushing them with boulders.

Redcaps will die if their caps dry out, so they must kill frequently, drinking the blood of their victims and using it to dye their caps. Even though they carry heavy iron spears and wear iron shoes, redcaps can outrun humans. You could escape one, however, if you quoted something biblical.

The Bad Luck of the Irish

Leprechauns are sprites or fairies found only in Ireland. They usually took the form of older men who were shoemakers by trade. And while they are considered mostly harmless to humans, they are notably taciturn and unsociable, so they usually live alone in remote areas. Until the twentieth century, leprechauns dressed in red, not green, which is the common belief today.

Leprechauns are reputed to be very rich, so there was always the temptation to capture one and force him to reveal where his gold was hidden. A leprechaun is a wily foe, though, so there are many tales about how he can trick a captor into unwittingly setting him free. In one popular old story, a boy ties a ribbon around a plant that marks a leprechaun's buried treasure. The boy makes the leprechaun promise not to remove the ribbon while he gets a spade. When the boy returns, the leprechaun has kept his promise, but he has also tied every other plant with an identical ribbon.

If you see a leprechaun and want to keep him in view, you must hold your gaze steady. He cannot escape until you take your eye off him, when he will vanish in a blink.

Clurichauns are less-known Irish fairies. They are always drunk and seen at night, which is why some folklorists think of them as leprechauns who have been out drinking after work. Clurichauns are bad-tempered and unfriendly, but it's worthwhile to always treat them well because they have a special interest in any wine you may own. If you're nice to a clurichaun, he'll look after it; treat him badly, and he'll ruin it and everything else in your house.

Leprechauns and clurichauns are believed to be so surly because they are the descendants of the inhabitants of Ireland who were displaced and banished by the invasion of the Celts.

Pixies

Pixies, also known as piskies, are little people with pointed ears who wear green clothing and pointed hats, and sometimes leave traces of pixie dust in their footprints. Even today, there is still a strong belief in pixies in Cornwall, England.

Pixies are thought to be:

- souls that failed to get into heaven, but were not bad enough to deserve hell
- mischievous and enjoy playing tricks on people
- borrowers of horses so they can ride at night
- the causes of travelers going astray
- cooperative—they will sometimes clean a house rather than mess it up if they are treated well and receive food or saucers of milk
- able to cast a spell on you if you upset them; however, turning your coat inside out will confuse them long enough to enable you to make your escape
- unable to touch silver because it burns their skin and will kill them if any gets into their blood

Fairies force young men and women to dance through the night, so they waste away. This was sometimes believed to be the cause of consumption, or tuberculosis.

Elves

There are many similarities in the superstitions associated with elves and fairies. The terms are often used interchangeably, but there are distinctions.

Elves were once regarded as nature or fertility gods who were believed to be as strong and handsome as humans and about the same size. Elves could intermarry with people, however, and any offspring with elvish blood were thought to be more beautiful than ordinary men and women. It was also believed that famous and powerful men such as kings could become elves after they died.

Similar to fairies, elves made circles where they danced, leaving behind mushroom rings or a circle of flattened grass. Treading over or damaging an elf ring was bad luck, and you could expect to fall ill. It was common for elves to cause pain and sickness, and the most common ailment was a rash called an "elven blow."

In Iceland, roads may still sometimes be rerouted or building plans changed if it is thought they will disturb rocks where elves are believed to live.

The name "elf" is Germanic in origin, and the belief in elves is common to most Germanic tribes and countries. Scandinavian elves had fair hair and skin. You could protect yourself from malevolent elves with a star-shaped elf cross. This was painted on doors and household items, or carried as an amulet. Even the worst elves could be appeased if you offered them food they liked, such as butter. This was traditionally placed inside a rock carving, known as an "elven mill."

An *Albtraum* (elf dream) is the German word for "nightmare." In a superstition similar to the Scandinavian belief in the "mara," it was believed that nightmares happened when an elf sat on your chest.

According to one Icelandic historian of the Middle Ages, there were two kinds of elves. Light elves were as bright as the sun, and lived in the sky's Elf Home, just below the home of the gods. Dark elves were black, and lived in the earth, where they worked in forges. They were either known as dwarves or related to them.

Dwarves

Early dwarves in Norse mythology were more or less the same height as humans, and had characteristics that superstitious people linked with death because they had pale skin and dark hair, and lived underground. They came out only at night and could by killed by sunlight. But as time went on, dwarves evolved to become magical, mysterious, short, ugly, and often comical. They were also metalworkers capable of making items of legendary value. Rumpelstiltskin, of the Brothers Grimm fairy tale, is a good example of this—he could spin straw into gold.

Gnomes

"Gnome" is a common term used to refer to a group of related sprites such as the Swedish tomte, the Prussian kaukis, the German kobold, the Swiss barbegazi, and the Dutch Kabouter.

The Dutch believed that the Kabouter usually lived underground or in mushrooms, while the Swedish tomte were helpful household spirits. But all gnomes were believed to be very small, perhaps only 2 inches (5 cm) tall. They were commonly depicted in traditional fairy tales as old men who wore long beards and pointed red hats, and lived underground guarding buried treasure.

Fairies love to steal babies and replace them with changelings, who grow up ugly, strange-looking, or physically afflicted. Luckily, a coat hung upside down nearby protects babies from this fate.

Goblins and Hobgoblins

The goblin is a bad-tempered, evil—and sometimes simply mischievous—character who ranges from child-sized to adult height. Many sprites in other cultures would be referred to as goblins in English.

British goblins are nomadic, moving constantly between dwellings in the roots of trees or clefts in rocks. Hobgoblins are very similar to goblins, but they are more likely to be friendly and amusing.

If goblins move into your house, you might wake up to find your furniture moved and your nightclothes stolen.

Kobolds

In Germany, there is a traditional belief in kobolds, who have the same origin as goblins. There are two types: One lives underground in mines, and the others are domestic sprites. Domestic kobolds can be helpful or play tricks on a house's residents, depending on their mood.

The underground kobold is like a dwarf, and is short, bent, ugly, and swarthy. He is related to the Welsh coblynau and the English knocker, both of which have small, thin limbs and a hooked nose. Some people once thought they actually lived in rock, the same way humans live in air, and there were mixed opinions about whether they were good or malevolent.

Superstitious miners claimed to hear kobolds mining for metal. Some people interpreted the knocking sounds as a warning to keep away from danger, and when miners remained safe, they were grateful to the kobolds. At times, miners followed the knocking, believing the sounds came from kobolds who were indicating where good veins of metal could be found.

In medieval times, kobolds were blamed for mining accidents and rockslides, and people prayed for protection from them. Miners also blamed the kobolds if the ore they mind turned out to be worthless. Some miners tried to bribe the kobolds with gold and silver, but this apparently only made them play more tricks. The metal cobalt was named after the kobolds because its ore can harm other metals, just as kobolds could harm people who didn't treat them well.

Some legends say domestic kobolds come and go through the chimney. They might appear as animals, fire, household objects, or a fiery stripe that flies through the air. You had to beware when taking in a wet cat or dog out of pity because it might be a disguised kobold, which could change form and stay forever. Much of the time, however, kobolds remained invisible to humans; however, if you wanted to trick one into becoming visible, you could trip it by throwing peas onto the floor or spread ashes on the ground to see its footprints.

If you try these tricks, be prepared for a very angry kobold. There's a tale of a man who did the latter and was killed, chopped into pieces, roasted, and eaten by the kobold. If you

Kallikantzaroi

A kallikantzaros (plural: Kallikantzaroi) is a Greek or Cypriot goblin that lives underground, sawing away at the roots of the World Tree to make it collapse and destroy the Earth. The World Tree is found in several mythologies and folk traditions, from Mesoamerica through Northern Asia to Norway. Its immense branches and roots connect the heavens, Earth, and the underground.

During the winter solstice, when the sun is farthest from the planet, the kallikantzaroi come to the surface. In the Northern Hemisphere this is around December 21st, but modern folklore fixes the kallikantzaroi's appearance between Christmas Day and January 6th, also known as Twelfth Night. When the kallikantzaroi return underground, they discover that the World Tree has healed, and they must begin the task of sawing through it all over again.

Kallikantzaroi are active at night, and cause all sorts of accidents and misfortune. To protect yourself, you could distract them by leaving a colander on the doorstep, where they would sit counting the holes for hours. Or you could leave the fire burning all night to protect your house. One long-standing superstition says a baby born during Saturnalia week, from December 17th to 23rd, was liable to grow into a kallantzaros. This fate could be avoided by singeing the baby's toenails, or binding them with garlic or straw.

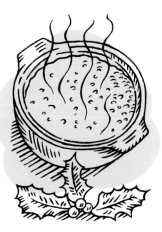

are prepared to treat one well, by leaving food and drink at the same time and place each day and generally respecting your housemate, a kobold could be a great help. So, if you find woodchips on the floor and dirt in your milk, it is a kobold announcing himself. If you leave the woodchips and drink the milk, the kobold will stay.

Household Sprites—Farm Hands

In Scandinavian folklore, the tomte, or nisse, is a house sprite that took care of a farmer's home and children when he was asleep. It was typically a little old man, usually with a beard and dressed like a farmer. These sprites were believed to be invisible, but able to change shape. A tomte was usually pleased with a bowl of porridge on Christmas night. Tomte were easily offended, however, and they disliked any change in farming tradition, as well as rudeness, swearing, and any unkindness to animals.

Never step on Saint-John's-wort. A fairy horse may rear up under your feet and take you on a wild and dangerous overnight ride.

Despite his small size, the tomte was extremely strong. For a minor offense, you may be knocked on the head; for a major one, he could kill your stock and ruin your fortune. He particularly cherished the farm's horses, and his favorite horse was always treated well. He would even braid its mane and tail. Usually, the braids seemed more like tangles, but traditional lore said it was very unlucky to undo them.

Accordingn to ancient belief, tomte was believed to be the soul of the first owner of the farm, who was usually buried somewhere on the land. Therefore, leaving food for a tomte can also be seen as remnants of earlier rites of ancestor-spirit worship. In more modern times, a successful farmer's reputation could be ruined by accusations that his tomte was stealing from nearby farms or doing "ungodly" work.

Brownies

Brownies or urisks are home-based sprites—the Scottish and English equivalent of the Scandinavian tomte. At one time, many manor houses had a seat close to the kitchen fire that was always left free for the brownie—just in case. People with the gift of second sight were among the few lucky enough to see brownies. You really should try to look after them, however, as brownies will:

- help around the home in exchange for food or gifts
- leave if they are treated badly
- leave if their gifts are referred to as payments, which they take as a slight
- work at night, when they cannot be seen
- make themselves visible only very rarely
- always be especially pleased with gifts of milk or cream
- rarely talk to humans
- meet other brownies near a stream or running water, where superstitious people believed that they could hear their chatter

Placing your shoes with the toes facing away from the bed will help to keep you safe from fairies at night while you sleep.

Imps

Imps are usually described as small, mischievous, but not malicious beings. They are like fairies and demons, but not as important. Being an imp could be lonely, which is what made them want to please—until they could no longer restrain their impishness. In the Middle Ages, some people believed imps were the familiar or animal spirits of witches who were kept locked in gemstones or containers, and magically called up when needed.

Woodland Spirits—Leszi

Similar to many woodland spirits around the world, the Russian leszi protects the forest and its animals. He is usually tall and appears human. However, he also:

- can change his size, shape, and form at will
- has hair and a beard of grass or vines
- can have a tail, hooves, and horns like a faun
- is often seen with bears and wolves
- when in human form, is discovered by his glowing, usually green eyes and shoes that are backward or on the wrong feet.

The Curupira, a South American woodland spirit, also has backward-facing feet, which confuse anyone following his tracks.

The leszi is mischievous and removes signs from their posts to confuse people. He can lure an unwary person to his cave by imitating the voice of a friend. Once in his lair, the leszi may tickle the captive to death. If you met a leszi, you were advised to immediately turn all of your clothes inside out, put them on backward, and move your shoes to the wrong feet. If you couldn't manage this before the leszi begins his torment, you had to set the forest on fire and run away as fast as possible. The leszi would be so preoccupied with saving his beloved forest and animals that he would forget you were ever there.

Water Spirits—Kappa

In Japan, water spirits called kappa are believed to inhabit ponds and rivers. Although some are friendly and helpful to people, most are troublemakers. Their nastiest tricks include looking up women's kimonos, stealing crops, and kidnapping and eating children. Kappa have webbed hands and feet, and a liquid-filled depression on the top of their heads. Their amazing strength depends on this liquid, and the best way to defend yourself from a kappa is to get them to spill it. Luckily, kappa are extremely polite. Superstitious Japanese parents teach their children to bow frequently, so the kappa will have to bow in return, spilling the liquid from their heads. The only type of food kappa love more than children is cucumber. Parents will write the name of their offspring on the skin of a cucumber before throwing it into water that is believed to be infested with kappa. Hopefully, this would satisfy their hunger.

Aircraft Spirits—Gremlins

Gremlins are spirits who sabotage aircraft and are often blamed for accidents during flights when no other explanation seems possible. The term was invented, and the creatures first seen, during World War I. Many aviators with the British Royal Air Force swore they had spotted gremlins interfering with crucial controls and equipment during a flight, just before things started to go wrong. It's likely that the gremlins and the accidents were caused by hallucinations due to stress and high altitude.

What a Nightmare!

In Scandinavian folklore, a mara, or mare, is a female wraith who causes nightmares by sitting on a sleeping person's chest. In Norwegian, Danish, and Icelandic, the word for nightmare translates as "mare-ride," and as "mare-dream" in Swedish. A mara may also ride horses at night and leave them sweating and exhausted by the morning—just as fairies and witches allegedly behave. She could also tangle your hair, the coats and tails of animals, or the branches of trees. Maras were once explained as the spirit of a sleeping woman that had left her body, either because she was wicked or because she was cursed. The cure was simple once you realized who was giving you nightmares: You would confront her and repeat three times, "You are a mara."

Omens

When something unusual happens, particularly in nature, superstitious people often associate it with an event that follows soon afterward and ascribe a link between the two. Unseasonal weather and odd behavior by animals are two common sources of good and bad omens. Since ancient times, people have taken note of signs that they believe will foretell good or bad luck, or predict something major, such as a death. Unusual celestial sights, such as comets and meteors, are often seen as very significant. However, even simple everyday encounters with other people or the activities of domestic pets can be ominous.

Nature Knows

Some people acquire their own personal omens. The great Italian tenor Luciano Pavarotti, for example, always looked for a bent nail in the backstage scenery before each performance, then slipped it into his pocket for luck. Bent nails are a common talisman among Italian singers. If Pavarotti found one—and it had to be from backstage—he believed that he would sing well.

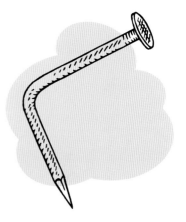

Something like this can, of course, become a self-fulfilling prophecy. Very often the prophesied outcome—in this case, good or bad singing—occurs because of the positive or negative attitude of the person rather than the actual omen itself. And that may be true of many superstitions.

If someone hits a drinking glass and it rings, it must be quickly stopped to save a sailor from drowning at sea.

When Plants Speak

Some superstitious people believe that the condition of plants and trees can predict future circumstances, for example:

- A tree carrying both fruit and blossoms at the same time foretells a death in the family.
- Giving or receiving parsley is an omen of death.
- Oak and ash trees are said to predict the coming season: If the first leaves to unfurl belong to the oak, summer will be mostly fine; if the ash is first, it will be a wet one. Even with modern science, the unpredictability of weather means that this type of superstition lingers on despite all rational logic.

165

As the Clouds Roll By

Weather is also portentous in a number ways. Some superstitious people see the shape of clouds as a sign of the future—or at least the weather. High, scattered clouds are known as a "mackerel sky," and are seen as a sign that there will be no rain for the next 12 hours. Colored skies have their own place in the world of omens. A green sky seen through rainclouds means more rain is on the way; a green sky after sunset means gales. Red skies could be good or bad. If the sky was red in the evening, the next day's weather would be favorable. A red sky in the morning, however, meant battening down the hatches and preparing for bad weather.

Red sky at night, sailor's delight,
Red sky at morning, sailor take warning.

Lights in the Sky

The northern lights or Aurora Borealis, for many people who live in the Northern Hemisphere who can see them, are said to be symbolic of war and death. And when they are at their most spectacular, it is a sign that a great war is either underway or about to begin. In the early part of 1939, when World War II was looking likely but not inevitable, the Aurora Borealis was seen as far south as London, which was very unusual. Many superstitious people interpreted this as a bad sign. Also just prior to the attack on Pearl Harbor, there were three nights of amazing displays in the United States, which were visible as far south as Cleveland, Ohio.

Based on this logic, it would seem that an eclipse of the sun would also be seen as a great portent. Eclipses do engender a vague feeling of doom among superstitious people; however, there does not seem to be a particular meaning assigned to them.

Today, rainbows are mostly regarded as positive symbols on which we can make a wish, or follow to find a pot of gold. And in Somerset, England, in 1925, it was believed that someone who saw three rainbows would be rich and lucky later in life. On the other hand, in parts of Scotland and Ireland, a rainbow with both ends on the same island, or the same town, foretold a death. And it is still believed in some places that it is bad luck to point at a rainbow, the moon, or stars. This may stem from a time when celestial bodies were seen as gods, and pointing at them was disrespectful.

Shooting Stars

Comets in the sky are commonly believed to herald great events. For example, Halley's comet, which returns every 76 years, appears in the Bayeux Tapestry that records William of Normandy's invasion of England in 1066. It is likely that the vision of the comet was seen as a good omen—to the Normans, certainly!

Storms and shooting stars could reflect the deaths of ordinary people, especially if they were extremely good—or bad. But comets marked the deaths only of important people. As Shakespeare wrote in *Julius Caesar* (1599):

When beggars die there are no comets seen;
The heavens themselves blaze forth the death of princes.

Lucky Bugs

Although they are commonplace, insects have a wealth of superstitions attached to them that often relate to their movements in and around people and houses. For example, if a bee lands on your head, you will be a great man or woman.

Killing a cricket will bring bad luck or death.

Crickets in the kitchen are generally lucky, especially if they sing and sit in the hearth. However, in other superstitions, crickets chirping or leaving a house where they have been for a while can foretell death. Flies coming into the house out of the usual season can mean death, too. Beetles are unpopular, and are often thought to bring misfortune, so they are always killed on sight. However, according to some superstitious people, killing beetles either brings rain, or means you will break a bowl. So you may want to think twice before stomping out a beetle.

If your geese cackle late at night, your house will be robbed.

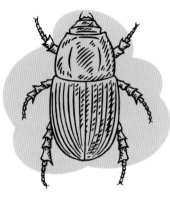

Even the humble caterpillar was once feared. Children often thought they were poisonous. However, there was some justification; there are several species that can irritate the skin if handled. If anyone was brave enough to pick one up, and it curled around a finger, forming a ring—that person was sure to die.

Winged Omens

There are many portents and signs associated with birds that foreshadow the future.

The First Cuckoo of Spring

Hearing the first cuckoo of spring has many powerful superstitions attached. Depending on where you are standing when you hear it, superstitious people might tell you different things: whatever you are doing at the time will form your main occupation for the rest of the year. As mentioned in Chapter Two, if you are in bed, it is very bad news indeed. If you are standing on a hard surface you will have a hard year. This is sometimes more extreme: If you are standing on grass, you will live, but if you are standing on stone or bare earth, you might die. The direction from which the call of the cuckoo reaches you may also make a difference. If the cuckoo is in front of you, for example, you will go up in the world. Some people believe that the direction from which the call comes is the direction toward which you will travel yourself, or from which a future lover will come. The superstitious also believe that seeing a cuckoo before you hear it means you will discover hidden secrets of some kind.

- A bird appearing at the window or entering the house is bad luck and may mean death, especially if someone in the house was already sick, and the bird is black.
- Finding a dead bird, or having one drop out of the sky in front of you, is considered unlucky. On the other hand, it is lucky if bird droppings land on you, although this may have developed as a way to comfort the unfortunate target.
- Keeping the eggs of wild birds in the house was unlucky, too. And even in the days when boys often collected them, their parents would often not allow them to be kept in the house.
- A cock crowing in the afternoon could mean that rain was coming. If it was raining when the cock crowed, good weather would appear the remainder of the day.

Pigeons were said to be the last food an invalid would want to eat. Therefore a desire to eat pigeon forecast a sick person's death.

Many people today still see crows and other large black birds as unlucky. Three crows seen together bode particularly bad luck. Oddly, but perhaps because of their rarity, white crows are even more unlucky than black ones. Grackles or jackdaws are also signs of death to come.

Pussycats and Prophecy

Cats, with their air of mystery, feature in many superstitions:

- Cats born in May were once believed to be unlucky, and to have a tendency to bring snakes and other undesirable creatures into the kitchen. Sadly, in previous centuries, it was common to drown, or otherwise dispose of, a litter of kittens born in May.

One For Sorrow…

In parts of Europe, magpies were once thought to be witches in an unhuman form. Some writers have referred to the magpie as the devil's bird. In truth, it is difficult to say why so many negative superstitions have grown up around this bird. One magpie seen alone is particularly unlucky. In some beliefs, the person receiving the misfortune only has to spot the magpie; in others it has to approach from a particular direction, hop, fly in front of him or her, or chatter near the house. In almost all cases, it is seen as the harbinger of bad news or death. However, there are exceptions. Some people still think a magpie perching on their roof brings good luck. And more than one magpie can bring good news, such as in this well-known English rhyme:

> *One for sorrow,*
> *Two for joy,*
> *Three for a girl,*
> *Four for a boy,*
> *Five for silver,*
> *Six for gold.*
> *Seven for a secret never to be told.*

Another common variation also contains a mix of good and bad fortune:

> *One for sorrow,*
> *Two for mirth,*
> *Three for a wedding,*
> *Four for a birth,*
> *Five for heaven,*
> *Six for hell,*
> *Seven you'll see the devil himself.*

Luckily for the superstitious, there are ways of counteracting the bad luck, if the number foretells an undesirable outcome. The methods include spitting, speaking either defiantly or politely to the bird, showing it respect by, for example, tipping your hat or bowing, and sometimes a combination of these steps. Luckily for the magpie, the worst thing to do would be to harm it, so in past times, the bird enjoyed an early form of protected status.

- A cat sitting with its back to the fire is said to predict snow or at least cold weather. If a cat washes behind her ears, it will soon rain.
- If a cat washes behind its ears, a stranger will come, and the first person a cat looks at after washing its ears will receive a letter.
- Black, and in some cases, white cats may be lucky or unlucky. It depends on where you live, whether you own them or meet them, whether or not they cross your path, and how many are involved.
- Dreaming of cats was once considered unlucky, predicting quarrels or subterfuge among friends.

Unusually playful or excitable activity in a cat tells of a storm to come.

- In the nineteenth-century, the death of a cat in the house was an ill omen for the household. Therefore, many beloved pets that fell ill were taken outside to either recover or die. It was believed that a cat with a cold would transfer the illness to the family and, again, it was often put outside.
- Some people thought a cat's sneeze was an omen of rain or, if it sneezed the day before a wedding, foretold a happy married life.

Sometimes the Bark Is Worse Than the Bite

A howling dog was once a sign of death to come, particularly if it was close to the house of a person who was ill, and especially at night. If the dog howled three times, the person was already dead. Being followed by a dog or a dog coming into your house is lucky. If your own dog won't follow you, however, that's unlucky—and annoying if it is the last walk of the night. A dog crossing the route of a funeral or coming between the couple at a wedding was definitely unlucky.

Fateful Foals

If a mare in foal is used to pull a funeral cart either she and her foal or a member of the owner's family will die within the year. Other people believe when you see the first young of a foal, or sometimes another young animal, you can predict whether you will have a good or a bad year. If the head is toward you, it will be good; if you see the tail, it will be bad.

Everyday Predictions

Unusual Encounters

When setting out on a journey or undertaking a new task, in medieval times, it was considered unlucky to meet a pig, hare, magpie, cat, or certain kinds of people, including women—particularly red-haired women, or those with bare feet or flat feet—nuns, members of the clergy, or unattractive people of either sex. However, the potential misfortune could be lifted if you spit over your left shoulder or at least crossed your fingers.

Depending on your beliefs, meeting a funeral could mean that the next person to go would be the same, or the opposite, sex as the person whose coffin you just met. But you could walk with the funeral party to avoid any disastrous consequences. In fact, some people thought it was polite to do so, for the funeral party's, and their own, peace of mind.

Meeting a funeral was an obvious sign of another death to come.

Someone's Coming

There are many omens that predict that a visitor will arrive, which must have been a more common occurrence in the days before telephones and email. Some signs include:

- A bee flying into the house
- A cock crowing at the door
- Getting your words mixed up
- Accidentally leaving the lid off a teapot

If you knock your elbow on something, you'll never sing again.

If a woman's skirt hem or a man's jacket hem is turned up, a present or letter is on its way for the wearer. However, the hem should not be flattened. Let it fall on its own; otherwise, the item will not arrive. A moth flying around the house means a letter, or some other form of news, is coming. And so does a spider, especially if you see it at night.

Magic Tickets

In mid-twentieth century Britain, children and young people believed that numbers on bus tickets could tell their future. There were a variety of ways to calculate the number, but many children added up the digits, and if they equaled 21, the ticket was lucky. In some cases, it then became a love token, and it was given to the person the child loved or liked. If the other person tore it and gave half back, it was a good sign. But if they threw it away, it was a bad omen.

However, if the numbers added up to a number other than 21, the ticket was still used to tell a fortune. The ticket owner would divide the number by 7 and use the remaining amount to match up with the "One for sorrow..." rhyme, usually used when seeing magpies.

Luck at Sea

It is a well-known superstition that it is unlucky for sailors to kill an albatross. In fact, many people think this is an ancient superstition. However, it seems to have surfaced after Coleridge's poem "The Rime of the Ancient Mariner" was published in 1798.

In an interesting twist, the idea has been extended to boxes of a brand of British matches, manufactured since 1861, known as Swan Vestas. It was reported as recently as 1994 that the swan pictured on the box represented the albatross in the poem and that anyone bringing a box onboard a fishing boat would bring bad luck with it. The consequences could be averted by throwing the box over the side of the boat, sailing around it three times, and returning to port before setting out once again.

In some locations, a bee landing on a ship brings good luck; in others it is believed to be a witch who will bring bad luck.

Sailors are often superstitious about things that may resemble a ship or boat. In some places, if a man sees his breakfast bowl turned upside down, he may not go to sea that day. And it is also extremely unlucky to lose a bucket overboard.

Too Much Fun

There are a few superstitions about excessive laughter, such as "laugh (or sing) before breakfast, you'll cry before supper," or "laugh till you cry, sorrow till you die." These sayings may relate to tempting fate, or simply result from the Puritan principle of condemning fun in general.

Itching and Twitching

A number of superstitions focus on different parts of the body itching. For example, if your elbow itches, you either will, or

Cats on ships had a practical purpose in keeping down rats. However, they were also considered lucky. Japanese sailors traditionally preferred a cat with three shades of fur, while Europeans preferred black cats. Most sailors believed that drowning a cat at sea was very unlucky. One superstition said it would create a storm; on the other hand, if there was no wind at the time, it might be considered favorable.

Even the humble clergyman was an ill omen for sailors. Meeting one on the way to the ship or boat, or when a fisherman was baiting his lines, boded ill, and the word "minister" was not spoken on board, in fear of ill luck. Likewise, meeting a woman with red hair was bad luck to many fishermen.

When people are abandoning a doomed project, they are often compared to "rats leaving a sinking ship." It was thought that when rats left home, they evacuated because they knew it would soon be in ruins. In 1889 three people working on the *Paris C. Brown*, a riverboat that sailed between Louisiana and Ohio, spotted some rats leaving the ship. They decided, on superstitious grounds, to leave the vessel, too. It proved to be a good decision: The *Brown* was never seen again, and nobody aboard it lived to tell the tale. It simply disappeared.

should, change your lover. Another belief suggests that if the inside of your elbow is itching, someone will soon come to your house; if it is the outside, someone will soon be leaving

For sailors, sneezing to the left means that the journey will be hard; to the right means that good weather will make their voyage a happy one.

Let Them Drown!

In the nineteenth century many people living in coastal areas around Britain would refuse to save a person from drowning; they might row or sail past the unfortunate person in the water, and even take anything that may allow them to save themselves, such as oars or buoys. People on the shore would watch as a person drowned in front of them. One superstitious reason for this was that it was said that, depending on whether the person was alive or dead, the person who brought the victim out of the water would be liable for the person's upkeep, or funeral. A second reason was that the rescued person would become an enemy and hurt or even  kill his or her rescuer. And a third reason was that the ocean would have its revenge on you for denying it that person's life, and take you instead at some later date. There is an element of "cheating fate" in all of these reasons. However, most superstitions involve a fatalistic attitude, where our destiny is determined by a chance occurrence or omen which we are powerless to change. Under this belief system, if the drowning person was destined to drown, the rescuer has interfered with fate and must somehow make up for their interference.

your home. Someone with itching feet will soon be walking on ground previously unknown to them. An itching right hand means money will soon be coming in: an itching left hand says money needs to be paid out. An itch on the nose means you will either kiss a stranger or meet a fool—although sometimes this is the other way around, too. If you shudder, especially when it is warm, people will often say someone or something is walking over your future grave.

Who Nose?

Nosebleeds were once thought to foretell bad luck—a superstition that dates back to at least the twelfth century.

An itchy right eye means laughter to come;
an itchy left eye means tears.

In parts of Scandinavia, there are two itching superstitions: If your head itches, you may expect bad weather; if your mouth itches, you can expect someone to punch it. If your itching nose causes you to sneeze once or twice, count how many and recite the following rhyme:

Once for a wish,
twice for a kiss,
three for a letter,
four for something better.

Or if you sneeze more than four times, you can consider an even number of sneezes to be unlucky and an odd number lucky. There are so many superstitions about the number of sneezes and when you might sneeze that it is impossible to draw any definite conclusions.

On the Face of It

Many people instinctively judge others by their looks. We try not to, but it is a persistent and irrational aspect of human nature. People whose eyes are close together may be seen as shifty, and those with wide set or large eyes seem innocent.

Hearing Things

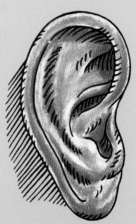

A very common superstition is that if your ear itches, tingles, or feels hot, it means that someone is talking about you. Usually a particular meaning is assigned to each ear, such as either your mother or your lover is talking. In general, if it is your right ear, someone is saying something good about you, and if it is the left ear, the words are bad. However, if the omen tells you its speaker is saying something bad about you, you can make the speaker bite his or her tongue or develop a stammer. Try pinching the offending ear, cutting off a piece of your apron or tying a knot in it, or biting a finger. But look out if you hear ringing in your ears; this predicts the death of someone close to you.

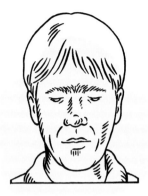

People with high foreheads are seen as innocent, too. However, this may stem from the fact that babies usually have high foreheads, so we extend their innocence to others with similar characteristics. On the other hand, many people mistrust a person whose eyebrows meet in the middle. An early reference to this appears in Thomas Lupton's *A Thousand Notable Things (1586)*, and speaks in no uncertain terms:

> *They whose haire of the eye-browes doe touch or meet together, of all other are the worst. They doe shew that hee or shee is a wicked person, and an enticer of servants, and given to unlawfull and naughty acts...*

An extra finger or toe is usually believed to be lucky.

Hair Lore

Hair can also reveal aspects of character. Those with curly hair, for example, are seen as proud. The hair does not have to be naturally curly; even people with straight hair can be tested by drawing a single hair quickly between two fingernails to see if it curls. Interestingly, the same test is done to see if riches will come to a person; if the hair curls, they will. Perhaps a sense of pride brings the riches, or vice versa.

Crooked Fingers and Webbed Feet

It may be worth taking care of your hands for more than personal vanity. Superstitious people are apt to read into their appearance. But there is not much you can do about the length of your fingers, which according to superstition, reflects a predilection for stealing. Crooked fingers mean the person will be generally bad toward others. However, if only the little finger is crooked, it predicts riches to come. Children have been known to pinch each other's little fingers to find out whether they could keep a secret. If the child cried out, they could not. Pulling on fingers to see how many joints cracked could predict almost anything you wanted, although most people tried this to find out how many sweethearts, or babies, they would have.

The size and shape of your toes may also be important. A woman whose second toe is longer than her big toe is in charge at home, but the same condition in a man suggests that he is cruel to his wife. Webbed toes are fortunate because they mean the person cannot be drowned!

Wear and Tear

Putting on an item of clothing inside-out brings good luck, as long as it is by accident, and you don't correct it for the whole day. If you mistakenly snap a needle in two while sewing, you'll have good luck. Snap it in three, and you'll soon have an offer of marriage. If your skirt catches in a doorway, it is a sign of bad luck to come. It is also bad luck for rats to gnaw on your clothes, and could foretell a death.

Don't step on a crack, or you'll break your mother's back.

Even the humble shoelace coming untied can be an omen of ill luck. This superstition, which still exists today, dates back to the twelfth century in England. Some people dress in the same order every day. A general rule of "right good, left bad" seems to apply, so that right things come first. And wear and tear on shoes appears in a rhyme from the late nineteenth century:

> *If you trip at the toe, you'll live to see woe.*
> *If you trip at the heel, you'll live to see a deal.*
> *Trip at the ball, live and spend all.*
> *Trip at the side, live to be a bride.*

Wardrobe Warning

If some of the foretold deaths actually come to pass and you wear mourning clothes, be sure to get rid of them after you

Can Clairvoyants See the Future?

Today, clairvoyants or fortune-tellers are often seen as light-hearted fairground entertainment. However, it was not long ago that people took very seriously those who said they could tell their fortune.

One interesting episode from 1920s England does offer mysterious evidence that there is some truth in fortune-telling. In 1922, a psychic researcher, Dr. Soal, took part in a séance with Blanche Cooper, a medium of the time. During the séance, he appeared to receive a message from an old school friend, named Gordon Davis. At the time, Soal believed Davis to have been killed while fighting in World War I. Perhaps understandably, therefore, he took the "message" seriously. In it, Davis apparently spoke of a house in half a street, with five or six steps and a half, and a dark tunnel beside it. The letter "E" was somehow important in the address. Opposite the house was something unusual, not a veranda, but something different from the other houses nearby. A room upstairs was described as having pictures of mountains and oceans, and a large mirror. Downstairs there were brass candlesticks and a black bird on the piano. Davis's message also mentioned a wife and son.

Three years after the séance, Soal found out that Davis was not, in fact, dead, but alive and living in Southend-on-Sea, Essex. He went to visit his friend, at 54 Eastern Esplanade (the important "E" appearing twice here as the initial letter), only to find that there were five steps and a small slab leading up to the house, a covered passage or tunnel beside it, and a covered shelter (the unusual feature) across the road. Indoors a pair of brass candlesticks and a china kingfisher were placed on the piano, and upstairs was a room with a large mirror and six pictures out of seven showing views of mountains and ocean.

Most of this detail might be said to be normal, but all of it taken together is quite a feat in terms of prediction. Even more creepy is the fact that the medium who had described the house had done so three years *before* Davis (and his wife and young son) had moved into the house.

wear them. Keeping them any longer is bad luck. And you should never wear mourning clothes when you are not in mourning, or you are asking for trouble.

White specks on fingernails are sometimes thought to predict gifts to come.

In Dreams

The meanings of dreams have been interpreted for centuries. Scientists still do not know how much relevance to give to them, or if there is a code to decipher them—although it seems unlikely. So we are left with many theories about what certain objects and events in a dream may mean. Many interpretations involve opposites: If a dream is about a wedding, it foretells a funeral and vice versa.

However, if you dream about eggs—which may represent life—turning rotten, someone close to you will die. Some people also believe if you dream on Friday and told someone about it on Saturday, the events would come true. You could also make a dream true by repeating it three times. Other superstitions say you should never tell your dreams before eating; the ideal plan was to first tell someone named Mary—although it wasn't clear whether you should do this if you wanted it to come true, or didn't.

Shoulder Blades and Sieves

Some people try to foretell the future with divination. In some cases, the scapula—shoulder blade—of a sheep, or some other animal, could be used. It would usually be boiled and the meat stripped away. Next, the "seer" would look at the dents and shape of the bone, and use them to see into the past and future—just like a clairvoyant in a fairground with a crystal ball.

In mid-nineteenth-century European farming communities, a common household sieve was used to predict who was going to die in the coming year. At midnight or another auspicious time, people took turns sieving, or riddling, husks of the grain.

The barn doors would be left open, and it was believed that while the person to die that year riddled, those present would see coffin bearers or another visual clue pass by the doors. From about the sixteenth to the nineteenth century, a sieve was also used to find out who stole an item. Shears were stuck into it, and someone would walk around a group of people, asking the shears to turn the sieve when it reached the thief.

If a hare runs through a town or village, there will soon be a fire in it.

Our Daily Bread

Since bread is a staple food, it is hardly surprising that it is involved in many superstitions. It is also symbolic of sustenance in general, so it was regarded with a degree of respect. Some beliefs include:

- If your bread rises well, your sweetheart is thinking kindly of you.
- If your bread breaks frequently while it is in the oven, it is a sign that a stranger will come to eat it.
- If four loaves should stick together while baking, a wedding is to come, but if five stick together, there will be a funeral.
- If you take three loaves from the oven at the same time, or drop a loaf while in the process, there will be a death within the year.
- If you burn bread, it is very bad luck.

Many people believe it is unlucky to slice bread, and that it should always be broken.

Russian tradition, on the other hand, says that it is lucky to slice bread, and unlucky to break it. If you do cut it, a crooked slice may mean a crooked or unlucky life to come. But an evenly cut loaf means success and wealth. And taking the last slice of bread from a plate—only when offered and never of your own accord—means you will have either a handsome partner or a single life, depending on whom you ask.

Knocking over a chair as you stand up is unlucky, though some people say it is a sign that you have been telling lies.

Chairs and Tables

Even basic household furniture is still seen as ominous today:

- Gamblers will sometimes stand up and turn their chair around in an attempt to better their luck.
- Turning your chair while speaking to someone indicates that you will quarrel.
- Creaking furniture means rain or death. Until recently, most of the furniture in homes would have been old and made of wood, and probably creaked a lot.
- To place certain objects, such as shoes or an umbrella, on a table is still believed to bring bad luck. When homes were heated solely by fire, placing a pair of bellows on a table was also risky, and usually meant there would be a fight or argument in the house.

Which Way the Candle Drips

Blowing or snuffing out a candle was another omen of death. If the wind blew out a candle on a church altar (or the light from the candles dimmed), it was likely that the minister would die. A candle that dripped on one side as it was being carried into a church also predicted death. Even the act of cutting a candle in two, presumably to delay buying more, could cause problems for superstitious farmers because something would go wrong with their cattle. But on a more positive note, if you spot a bright spark on a candle, you will

receive a letter soon. If you want to know when it will arrive, tap or hit the bottom of the candlestick, and the amount of times you have to do this before the spark falls off indicates the number of days.

Three candles burning on a table foretell a death at sea, a wedding, or a funeral.

Dropping, Spilling, and Falling

It is generally bad luck to drop, spill or break things, and while there are are too many to list here, the most popular superstitions refer to common household items. However, some items have a specific outcome associated with them. It is a well-known belief that breaking a mirror brings seven years' bad luck.

A picture falling from the wall for no obvious reason means death. If it is a portrait, it may mean the death of the person pictured, or a member of his or her family. Some people believe this applies only if the glass breaks. Hanging pictures above a door or bed was unlucky, perhaps because they might fall on someone passing through or sleeping. To trip or fall is unfortunate and generally unlucky, especially at the start of a journey or on stairs; although falling up stairs might foretell a marriage to come.

Salty Omens

Spilling salt was thought unlucky since at least the sixteenth century. Early references suggest that it was bad luck for the person that it spilled toward, rather than the spiller. Beginning in the eighteenth century, it was the person doing the spilling who needed to worry. However, they could avert the bad luck by throwing a pinch of the spilled salt over their left shoulder, into the fire, or both. But is not clear when it was first said that the devil lurked on or behind the left shoulder. This idea may have been invented to explain the superstition, rather than the other way around.

Why Shouldn't We Walk under Ladders?

Everyone seems to know the superstition that it is unlucky to walk under a ladder. But why? There are three main theories:

The least likely is that the ladder forms a triangle with the wall it leans against and the ground. Since Christians believe in the Trinity, walking through a triangle would be disrespectful. There is no evidence to suggest that this is the original meaning of the superstition, and it does seem far-fetched.

The second theory is also based on Christianity, but it refers to the ladder used to take Christ from the cross after his death. Some people say the devil was lurking there triumphantly, and trouble will come to those who walk through a triangle.

The third theory is that people who were about to die on the gallows had to climb up a ladder to get there. This does relate to earlier references that claim walking under a ladder would lead to death by hanging. Therefore, it would seem logical that climbing a ladder that would become a superstition, rather than walking under one, but superstitions are not known for making sense.

The earliest clear reference to the ominous nature of this superstition was that you would never marry if you walked under a ladder, and that does not seem to relate to any of the reasons above. Today, most people believe that bad luck will befall anyone who passes below a ladder. The most likely explanation is the most obvious—that something might fall on you. In 1881 the following account was published in *Punch* magazine:

> It is considered unfortunate by some people to go underneath a ladder. These are the people on whom workmen have dropped pots of paint and molten lead. Others consider it unfortunate to pass outside a ladder. These are they who have stepped off the pavement into the road and have been run over by traction-engines.

If you suddenly realize that you have walked under a ladder, there are a number of antidotes to undo the damage. Spitting between the rungs or crossing your fingers, is said to be effective. Or, if you are walking with someone else, you can wait for the other person to speak first, and the bad luck will transfer to that person instead of you.

Good Luck Charms

Throughout history, people have carried lucky charms, or placed them in their homes and workplaces. There are various types of good luck objects and each has a different function. The word "charm" comes from the Latin word for song, and it relates to chanting magical words, which result in enchantment. "Talisman," another word for a good luck charm, has its roots in the Greek word for an object that has been consecrated through a magical or religious ritual. In modern English it is usually something containing a written message or a symbol, which brings good luck.

Lucky Symbols

Talismans can sometimes protect their owner from harm. Overall, when situations seemed unsure or scary, people have looked for something that will bring them confidence and ultimately, good luck.

Four-Leaf Clovers

No other plant seems so lucky as the four-leaf clover, and in the United States alone, approximately 4 million are sold each year. It has been a good luck symbol in Britain since at least the sixteenth century. The ordinary three-leaf clover is considered lucky, especially in Ireland, where it is called a shamrock, so it is hardly surprising that the rare four-leaf version is even luckier.

Carry a double nut for luck, but never eat both kernels.

There are a variety of meanings attributed to the three-leaf clover, including the Triple Mothers of Celtic tradition—maiden, mother, and crone). And there is the tale told of how St. Patrick converted the Irish people to Christianity by using the shamrock to demonstrate the three-in-one qualities of the Holy Trinity.

The three-leaf clover is also known to stand for faith, hope, and love. If there is a fourth leaf, it stands for luck. However, the four-leaf version is also believed to stand for fame, wealth, a faithful lover, and health. It was once thought to have protective properties against the evil eye and witchcraft, and to allow the carrier to see through the tricks of fairies or malicious people. Today it is usually carried for good luck.

187

Amber

Amber, the fossilized resin of pine trees, has traditionally been worn as a jewel and a charm to ward off bad luck and attract the good. Like so many items connected with superstition, an absence of knowledge and an attempt to make something already rare and expensive seem even more mysterious helped to create many explanations for what amber was and where it came from. Some theories included that it was the solidified urine of the lynx, or the tears of the Norse goddess Freya, or of birds. In Greek mythology it was believed that when Phaeton, son of the sun god Helios, was killed, his sun-nymph sisters were turned into trees. Every year they wept for his death and their tears became solid amber.

Heather is generally unlucky in the house. But white heather is lucky.

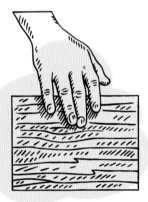

Touching Wood

Wood is rarely carried as a good luck charm, but the act of touching wood can be lucky. After saying something we want to happen or wish to avoid happening, even today, many of us still say, "Knock on wood!"—even if there is no wood in sight—so that we don't "tempt fate." The earliest reference to touching wood dates back to an early nineteenth-century children's tag game where touching wood made the player "safe." In another version of this game, the players were safe when they touched anything iron.

Lucky Beans

The ocean can carry the fruits, seeds, and beans of plants growing close to the coast to far-off destinations. When they drift ashore, and people find these unfamiliar, exotic objects, they are often called lucky beans. People carry them in pockets, or sometimes make them into necklaces.

Hot Luck

In Italy, animal horn pendants were popular good luck charms for centuries, but when red chili peppers were first introduced from South America, people thought they looked like the horn pendants, and began to hang them in the kitchen as good luck charms, as well as using them for cooking. From the kitchen, they spread into the rest of the house, shops, and cars. Modern synthetic versions, which are an amalgamation of the original animal horn and the chili shapes, are now available. They are popular throughout Italy and in countries with a large Italian population, such as the United States.

Bent Coins

Some people believe it is unlucky to find money in general or to pick it up if you do find it. However, discovering a bent coin has been said to be lucky since at least the sixteenth century. These were often coins that had been dropped and run over by a cart, or more recently, a car or another vehicle. A later superstition, from the nineteenth century, included coins with holes as lucky, too.

In medieval times, bent coins were sometimes offered to saints at shrines when people prayed or made a vow.

Charming the Cards

It should not be a surprise that superstitions abound in games of chance. Gamblers in particular were known for their susceptibility to lucky practices and charms of all kinds. A length of rope from a gallows was once a popular talisman, but many gamblers invent their own good luck tokens. For example, some people carry a coin that was minted in the year they were born.

Animal Auspices

Lady Luck

The ladybug, known as a ladybird in some English-speaking countries, enjoys unusual popularity for an insect. Other bugs are often squashed, but the ladybug is encouraged to fly away free. Its reputation for bringing good luck is almost certainly the main reason for this, plus it is extremely bad luck to kill a ladybug. Some of the numerous superstitions include:

- In Canada, ladybugs wintering in your garage are considered good luck.
- A medieval European tradition said that ladybugs were sent from heaven to rescue crops because of their noteworthy ability to curb pests in gardens, orchards, and farms. For this reason they were referred to as Our Lady's beetle—Our Lady referring to the Christian Virgin Mary.
- On English farms, seeing a ladybug foretold a good harvest.
- In France the sight of a ladybug meant good weather.
- If a ladybug lands on your hand, it is considered a blessing as long as you do not brush it away. The redder the ladybug, the better your luck will be. The number of spots on the ladybug foretells the number of happy months ahead. When it flies off, probably to escape the heat from your hand, your future love will come from the same direction in which the ladybug departs.

Rabbit's Foot

People were once much less sympathetic to animals than we are today, and they have been very ruthless toward animals if they thought it would do themselves some good. Rabbits' feet, particularly the back ones, were once popular in Britain as lucky charms. The earliest reference dates back to 1827, but there are few references after that until well into the twentieth century, when the foot is usually a rabbit's rather than a hare's. In the United States the rabbit's foot is still one of the better known lucky charms. It is possible that the lucky rabbit's foot may have been introduced to, or at least popularized in, North America from Britain, perhaps during World War II. Here are some reasons why these feet give people the courage to carry on:

■ Hares are often described as unlucky and not suitable for eating. Some people even believed they were witches in disguise. Stories were sometimes told of a hare that had been shot, but not killed, running into a house. When the hunter followed it inside, he would see a witch tending to her wound in exactly the same place that the hare had been wounded. Therefore, possessing a hare's foot was proof that a witch had been killed.

An acorn doused with musk oil and carried in your pocket or in a charm bag will attract the opposite sex.

All in the Bones

A variety of bones were once popular as good luck charms, including a T-shaped bone from a sheep's skull and a round bone from a pig's skull. The wishbone from a chicken or turkey—the bird's Y-shaped collarbone—is often copied for necklaces or lucky charm bracelets. Traditionally, in order to get the wish, the bone is dried for three days to make it brittle. The dried bone, sometimes called a "merrythought," is given to two people to pull apart. Each person crooks a little finger around one of the two ends, pulling until the bone breaks in two. Whoever is left holding the larger part gets the wish. As in many wishing rituals, the wish must not be revealed if it is to come true. Some people think that the power of the wishbone lies in its shape, which resembles a lucky horseshoe. Others believe that it was originally taken from a sacrificed hen.

- Actors once used the foot of a hare or rabbit to apply face powder. When modern brushes were introduced, however, the actors were reluctant to get rid of the feet because they had seen them through so many stressful openings and other theatrical events. So they kept the feet for good luck.
- Hare's feet are popular charms for people in high-stress, high-risk occupations such as driving racecars and flying planes.

Because of the number of eggs they lay, frogs are seen as symbols of abundance, and some people carry model frogs with them for luck.

The Whole Hare

Meeting a hare was very unlucky. It was once believed that a pregnant woman meeting a hare would give birth to a baby with a harelip (cleft palate). Certain fishermen would not go to sea if they met a hare on the way to the boat. And according to records from as early as the seventeenth century, one of the earliest taboo words on a boat or ship was "hare." Most of the other recorded taboo words are only as recent as the nineteenth century.

Good Ganesha

The Hindu god Ganesha had the head of an elephant, and was said to bring success, wealth, and peace. At some point, Ganesha's qualities became attributed not only to the god but also to real elephants, and they were seen as symbols of good luck. Tiny charms in the shape of elephants became popular across the globe. By the 1920s and 1930s, an elephant was included on most charm bracelets in Europe and North America. The elephant was almost always depicted in a walking position, with its trunk raised and curled so that it was touching its forehead to keep the luck in. Elephant charms are no longer as popular, though, possibly because we are aware of the dwindling numbers of wild elephants, and to equate them with luck does not seem appropriate.

Japanese Beckoning Cat

The *maneki neko*, or Japanese beckoning cat, attracts good luck and wards off bad luck. If its right paw is raised, it is believed to invite money into the home. If its left paw is raised, it draws customers into a business. Its origin story takes place at a poor Buddhist temple, where the monks were close to starving, but still shared their food with the temple cat. One day some wealthy samurai arrived at the temple. The cat raised its paw as if beckoning them, and they followed it into the temple. As soon as they were inside, a storm began and lightning struck in precisely the same place they had just been standing. The cat had clearly saved their lives.

While the samurai were waiting for the storm to pass, they learned about Buddhism. Later one of them became a monk at the same temple. He left it a large estate, and his family was buried there. Close to their tombs is a small shrine to a cat, in memory of the beckoning cat.

> Because it was once a rare and valuable metal, finding iron of any kind was traditionally regarded as lucky.

The Hard Stuff...

One theory suggests that at one time, the main source of iron would have been meteorites—a gift from the gods—but this is really speculation. Today the luckiness of iron has been eclipsed by the luck of the horseshoe.

Horseshoes: Which Way Up?

The horseshoe is a frequent good-luck icon. It's believed to be lucky to carry a horseshoe, or even just the nails from a horseshoe, and to nail one above the door of a house or stable—a tradition that dates back to the late fourteenth century. Its original purpose was to protect the household or animals from witches. However, since the nineteenth century, it is regarded as generally lucky. The argument about which way to hang a horseshoe has been going on for centuries. Some people argue that if it is hung heel (open end) down, the luck falls out; others feel if it is hung the other way, the devil sat in it. It is unclear how the tradition started. There are theories that it used to represent a horned god, or the devil. But the most likely explanation is that iron was believed to repel both witches and fairies, and when horses were the main form of transportation, horseshoes were a readily available source of iron.

It was also much luckier to find a horseshoe than to buy one or get one from your own horse. Of course, we are much less likely to find a horseshoe today. So perhaps this makes it even luckier.

...and the Black Stuff

A piece of coal can also be a good luck symbol. If coal is found lying around, a superstitious person may pick it up and throw it over his or her shoulder or simply place it in a fire. However, coal was once commonly carried in pockets for luck, especially on days when a person thought it was really needed, such as during exams and driving tests. Fishermen often carried a lump of coal with them when going to sea.

Hunchback's Hump

In the nineteenth and twentieth centuries, the hunchback became a lucky charm in many parts of Europe; people believed that touching or rubbing a humped back brought luck. They were especially popular with people on their way to horse races, and some hunchbacks positioned themselves in train station entrances, where they would charge a small fee for allowing their backs to be touched. In Monaco, small figures in the shape of a hunchback called Gobbo were popular with gamblers in casinos located in Monte Carlo, and they would rub the hump before playing. In fact, the term "playing a hunch" originally meant making your play after touching a hunchback.

Some people carry models of pyramids to attract good luck, believing that pyramids amplify and then focus positive energy through its apex.

Figures of Fate

Hand of Fatima

One of the most popular lucky charms in the Middle East today is a stylized hand called the hand of Fatima. It may be hung on the wall of a house or worn as a pendant, when a smaller version is used. The hand commemorates a story about Lady Fatima, the daughter of Mohammed, who was cooking one day when she saw Ali, her husband, arrive unexpectedly with a young female companion. She was struck with shock but remained silent and went on with her work. Only when Ali rushed over to her shouting did she

195

Gemstones

Gemstones are believed to bring good luck for certain people, depending on when the person was born. There are a number of lists, but the most popular list provides some of the particular qualities that people believe the stones bring. The Jewelers of America officially adopted the following list in 1912.

January: garnet—faith, eternity, and truth
February: amethyst—wit and health
March: aquamarine—understanding and happiness
April: diamond—eternity, courage, and health
May: emerald—love, goodness, and fidelity
June: pearl—peace, nobility, and beauty
July: ruby—love, enthusiasm, and strength
August: peridot—peace and success
September: sapphire—truth and serenity
October: opal—purity, wisdom, and hope
November: topaz—wisdom, sincerity, and courage
December: turquoise—happiness and love

Alternatively, stones also represent the day of the week on which you were born.

Monday: pearl
Tuesday: garnet
Wednesday: cat's eye
Thursday: emerald
Friday: topaz
Saturday: sapphire
Sunday: ruby

realize that she was stirring the boiling hot food with her hand.

Sign of the Cross

The Christian cross may be the most well-known version of the cross today—with and without the figure of Christ. However, the cross has been one of the most common religious symbols since ancient times, and nearly all cultures have used crosses in one form or another as charms. The Christian cross was adopted from earlier versions, and many people initially objected to its use. The Egyptian ankh has been around for millennia. It may be based on a knot or bow, but has a definite cross shape. Also found in Egypt, as well as other parts of the Middle East and Western Europe, was a Tau, a T-shaped cross, that was often worn as a charm.

Simple crosses were popular in Cyprus as early as 4000 B.C. One theory says that they represented a woman with her arms outstretched—a simplified fertility symbol.

Say It Once, Say It Twice

Many people have traditional sayings that they believe work like a charm to bring luck for a period of time. On the first morning of each month, for example, it is common in many families to say "rabbits" or "white rabbits" three times.

In Hawaii it is believed that wearing a shark's-tooth pendant will bring good luck, protect against evil spirits, and protect surfers against accidents and shark attacks.

Some also say "hares" the night before or the other way around. This charm relates to superstitions about beginnings and luck: If you begin something well, it will end well. However, there isn't an answer as to why so many of the sayings involve rabbits and hares.

Fingers Crossed

People make all sorts of signs for luck. These are usually done with their hands, which are the part of the body most easily seen by the gesturer and by others, and also the most easily hidden.

The gesture may be related to the Christian cross, because it is mostly found in countries where Christianity is one of the main religions. Models of crossed fingers are also fashioned into jewelry in countries where it is a common sign.

European Christians identify the snake with Satan, leading self-styled social outcasts to use the snake as a good luck symbol.

A common sign in many countries is crossing your index and second fingers for general good luck; but sometimes it is done furtively behind your own back—for example, when you are not quite telling the truth.

An Andean Smoking God

In the Andes of South America, a very popular god of luck is the house guard Ekeko. Models or small statues of him with a humped back were originally made of stone, but these days he is usually seen in brightly painted ceramic, and without the hump. He brings good fortune and protection to the house.

Ekeko is often portrayed wearing traditional Andean clothing, including a poncho, and loaded with baskets of grain, food, money, and other valuable items. Although he was originally seen as a deity by the traditional people of Peru, Bolivia and northern Argentina, modern migrations of people to the cities of south America have seen Ekeko adopted as a superstition meant to bring good luck to a home.

Offerings of cacao leaves, alcohol, and a cigarette are brought to him. The cigarette is lit and placed in his open mouth. It is said that the more he "smokes" before the cigarette goes out, the better the household's luck will be in the coming year.

Ekeko is celebrated on January 24, when a shaman brings a new version of him to a house, blesses him, and hands him over to the householders. Miniature versions of the things the household would like him to help obtain during the year are also bought and hung on the statue.

Protective Amulets

We live in a world fraught with danger. Even with the benefits of modern medicine, we all get sick or injured from time to time. We may think that we are too sophisticated and understand the world too well to rely on "magical" items for protection. Yet an incredible number of people wear an ornament or piece of jewelry, often called an amulet, to ward off evil or disease.

Symbols of Safety

While some amulets serve as a reminder of religious beliefs, others have a symbolic meaning of another kind. The variety of these protective talismans, amulets, and mascots is astonishing.

Talismanic Plants

For centuries some trees and plants have been credited with powerful and useful attributes, including:

- Magicians who possessed wands made of ebony wood had the greatest power.
- Carrying fern could guide you to great treasures.
- Saint-John's-wort was known as the devil chaser by ancient Romans for its supposed power to keep away evil spirits.
- Wood from a rowan tree protected ships from storms and houses from lightning, and when used on a grave, prevented the spirit of the dead person from haunting the living.
- Because oak trees can live to 250 years or more, their acorns were credited with preserving youth and life. It was believed they could ward off cholera if worn or carried in pockets.
- An acorn placed on a window ledge protected the house from lightning strikes.

Islamic Talismans

Because followers of Islam must not create images of either Allah or the prophet Mohammed, their talismans rely heavily on the written word. The most popular are verses from the Koran, particularly Ayat al-Kursi or the Throne Verse. This is very long, so it must be written very small. However, devout Muslims know the words by heart and do not need to read them. A talisman that many Muslim parents give their children reads *Ma Shaa Allah* ("what God has willed"). Another is the two Holy Names: Allah and Mohammed.

Henna Night Parties

In many parts of Asia, the Middle East, and North Africa, a bride-to-be has henna patterns painted onto her hands and feet to protect her from evil spirits. The painting is done a few days before the wedding, on the henna night, which the bride usually spends with her female friends. This may be the origin of the term "hen night," used in some European countries for

Abracadabra

Long before the phrase "Abracadabra!" was adopted by stage magicians, it was used as a charm to cure ailments such as a toothache or ague (malarial and other fevers).

To activate the charm, it was usually written on paper or parchment as an inverted triangle. The first line was abracadabra, the next line cut off the first and last letter to read *bracadabr*, and so on:

```
a  b  r  a  c  a  d  a  b  r  a
   b  r  a  c  a  d  a  b  r
      r  a  c  a  d  a  b
         a  c  a  d  a
            c  a  d
               a
```

It can now be read in several directions, a curious phenomenon that has fascinated people for as long as humans could write. The abracadabra triangle is first recorded in English at the end of the seventeenth century, but it has been found in earlier classical works. The construction was usually worn on an amulet hung around the neck.

The word most likely originates from the ancient Babylonian phrase *Abbada Ke Dabra* meaning "perish like the word," which may refer to the triangular pattern. Or it could come from Hebrew words for the Holy Trinity: father (*ab*), son (*ben*), and holy spirit (*ruach acadach*). Nobody knows for sure, which makes it easier for cultures to acquire and interpret the word their own way.

a bachelorette party, where a bride-to-be celebrates with a party with her girl friends before her wedding.

After a ritual bathing, the woman sits with her eyes shut while a hennaria—usually a woman—paints the henna in intricate designs that often include stars and crosses. The bride's hands and feet are wrapped in embroidered bags to prevent the patterns from smudging while the henna dyes the skin overnight.

The ritual comes from the belief is that a happy wedding attracts evil spirits who wish to spoil it. The precise henna patterns give both the bride and groom extra protection from any spells that might be cast upon them.

Rats!

Rats and humans have been living together for centuries, but haven't been in comfortable cohabitation. One way to get rid of rats was to write the following charm on a piece of paper. It can be read in many directions, which is considered to be part of its supposed magical powers.

R A T S
A R S T
T S R A
S T A R

The catch was that the piece of paper had to be put into the mouth of the king of rats. Regardless, the charm was known in Wales well into the twentieth century.

Getting the Blues

In the early twentieth century in London and other parts of Britain people—particularly children in poor areas—wore blue beads as talismanic necklaces. These were meant to protect against colds, bronchitis, and other respiratory illnesses. The necklaces were not taken off at night or when bathing, because it was thought that even a moment without the beads would give the diseases a chance to take hold.

The trend lasted only from about 1909 until the 1930s. Some theories propose that the beads echoed an old belief that the color blue had healing powers. But no one knows the real reasons behind what might have simply started as a fashion craze.

Speak and Write No Evil

The power of words, particularly among those who could not read, has often been used as a charm. One of the most popular was "A Copy of a Letter by Our Savior Jesus Christ". Women wore this pinned inside their clothing as a general charm against illness and the pain of childbirth in particular. It was printed repeatedly in the newspapers, produced and sold cheaply in Britain from the sixteenth to the nineteenth centuries. These papers also featured ballads, gossip, speeches, political news, and religious material.

At a time when few people could read or write, spoken charms or cures were common. These were the opposite of chanted spells, which were usually meant to do harm.

Many spoken charms were related to Christian beliefs. A spoken cure from 1878 included two angels, and they came from the North. Someone affected by ringworm would hold a pinch of ash from a fire between his or her fingers and recite:

Ringworm, ringworm, red
Never mayest thou either speed or spread
But aye grow less and less
And die away among the ash.

Next the pinch of ash was thrown back into the fire.

Wearing Words

In Devon, England, in 1908, curiosity got the better of a young man who had worn a bag around his neck to prevent epilepsy for as long as he could remember. Because it seemed to work, the mother of a child who had begun to show symptoms begged him for the secret. So the bag was opened and it was found to contain pieces of paper, each with just one word written on it. Arranged in the right order, they said:

Sinner, Jesus died for Thee
Therefore flee that sin.

Hoping for Health

Eye for an Eye

Many superstitions rely on the premise that a sickness or condition can be cured by something that resembles its symptoms. This is often known as a "like-for-like" cure.

Spiders, for example, were used as amulets to cure the ague (fever). Shivering is a fever symptom; therefore a creature that gave someone the shivers was believed to counteract the symptom. One "cure" was to imprison a spider in a bag and hang it around the neck of the sufferer. Another method was to actually swallow a spider.

Pliny the Elder, the author, naturalist, and natural philosopher of ancient Rome, included a cure for ague in his book *Naturalis Historia (Natural History)*. In his version, a spider was enclosed in a reed and four of its grubs were placed in a walnut shell, and both were worn around the neck. As recently as 1879 it was believed that a spider in a goose's quill worked, too.

Other like-for-like cures include fire or something red for erysipelas (see below) and red cloth for scarlet fever. A

victim of scarlet fever would be clothed in red fabric, and such things in the sick room as bed linen and curtains might be changed to red, too. In the early twentieth century, some people still wore red flannel around their necks as an amulet against scarlet fever.

Erysipelas, or Saint Anthony's fire, is a bright red rash, usually on the face or legs, which feels very hot. Therefore, the like-for-like treatment was based on other red elements. In some cases blood from families thought to be charmed was rubbed onto the skin. Yet because the condition was likely to

The belief in like-for-like was the impetus for wearing a leg-shaped bead around your ankle to prevent the loss of a limb.

Better Red...

Many superstitions link red thread or material with protection against disease or evil:

- Worn around the neck, red thread was said to prevent nosebleeds, another example of like-for-like superstitions.
- Wrapped around a piece of rowan tree red thread protected against witches.
- Tied onto a cow's tail, red thread protected against the evil eye and elf-shot.
- For adults, a skein of red silk or ribbon around the neck prevented quinsy, an inflammation of the throat. If the patient was a man, some said that the silk or ribbon had to be tied in place by a maiden.
- Red thread was used against rheumatism, teething, sprains, and sometimes the pain of childbirth.
- Red thread tied around children's necks was said to prevent them from drowning.
- A red silk bag hung around the neck on red silk thread protected against illness and general harm.
- To settle the mind of a lunatic, you tied clove-wort around his neck with red thread when the moon was waning in April.

disappear on its own accord, almost anything could have been said to help. Sometimes a written charm was used: The victim's name was written around the edge of the red patches to prevent the rash from spreading.

Black wool was used to ward off sprains—perhaps because it matched the discoloration of a bruise. A "wresting thread" of nine knots was made of it, and it was wrapped around the leg or arm, often accompanied by a spoken charm as it was tied.

Clean Air Acts

In the Middle Ages, the noxious air of the universally unsanitary towns and cities was believed to be the cause of diseases, such as the Black Death. In an attempt to somehow to cleanse the air they breathed, the wealthy carried or wore pomanders of dried herbs and spices. Some were encased in perforated containers, while others were shaped like balls. A traditional pomander—often seen at Christmas—has small dried oranges studded with cloves. Another type has rings with a hinged bezel that opens to reveal a small cavity. When the smells were particularly bad, the pomander was placed close to the nose and probably masked the worst smells, if nothing else. They are usually used today to scent a wardrobe.

Garlic's protective qualities against vampires seems to be an invention of nineteenth-century novelists.

Garlic Breath

Subsequent twentieth-century movies promoted the myth of the efficacy of garlic even more. But like onion, garlic has a great efficacious medical use, including easing the symptoms of whooping cough, hemorrhoids, wounds, and animal or insect bites. So, it's not a huge leap for a novelist to use it as an interesting device.

A Proper Turn

Another way to avoid bad luck was always to turn "sunwise," or clockwise. This is the "correct" way. To turn the other way was "widdershins," and it was almost universally associated with bad luck. Even today, a decanter of port is always passed to the left at a table, so it moves the correct way.

- Superstitious fishermen—and that was most of them— would make a point of turning only clockwise. Even their rope would be coiled that way, although the way a rope is made gives it a natural tendency to coil in that direction.
- Twentieth-century cooks still exhort others to stir ingredients in only the clockwise direction, and others said stirring tea in the pot widdershins would cause quarrels.

Touched for the Very First Time

British and French kings were believed to cure scrofula, or tuberculosis of the lymph nodes, simply by touching sufferers. Also known as the King's Evil, belief in its royal cure continued from approximately the eleventh century to the early eighteenth century.

Special gold coins created to mark the touching ceremony were hung around the patients' necks as amulets to continue fending off the disease. These coins were subsequently sold as cures in their own right.

If the palace was not convenient, the touch of the seventh son of a seventh son was an alternative. Another choice was the skin of a toad's leg that was removed while it was alive. This was worn around the sufferer's neck and the toad was buried. As the animal died and decayed, so would the disease.

- Funeral processions traditionally turned clockwise when approaching the grave, and some circled the churchyard or grave three times.
- Starting in the late eighth century, superstitious brides would turn only in the correct direction on their way to meet their bridegroom. In a related belief, people during the sixteenth century said that witches always turned widdershins.
- Turning clockwise might be viewed as a remnant of ancient sun worship, but it's more likely to be the natural direction for anyone who's right-handed.

Crossing Out

Crosses are powerful symbols and are carried as lucky charms in many cultures. They were believed to be very effective in warding off bad luck and diseases. For example, just making the sign of the cross over your shoe could prevent and cure frostbite.

However, double-crossing also means treachery. If underworld associates of a London criminal put two crosses against his name because he had betrayed them in some way, they would turn him in to the police.

Teeth for Two

Starting in at least the seventeenth century, mothers hung a bag containing teeth around the neck of a teething baby to ease them through this uncomfortable period. The teeth could be from an animal, but they may have been the mother's baby teeth, which her own mother would have kept for just this purpose. However, the oldest and most popular item was coral, because it somewhat resembled teeth.

Other necklaces used for teething included glass beads, deadly nightshade berries, and elderberries.

The most inexplicable teething amulet was made of hairs from the cross on a donkey's back, which were tied up in a black silk bag, and hung around the child's neck.

By Gum!

In the eighteenth century, a mole's front paw was used as an amulet to ward off convulsions in children. But by the nineteenth and twentieth centuries it was believed to cure toothaches.

The right foot was used if the toothache was on the right, and a left one for the other. But some people said that the foot had to be cut off while the mole was alive, and the animal was left to die in its own time. This sort of belief was common: As the animal died, so would the toothache.

A less grisly protection against toothache was to cut your fingernails and toenails before the sun rose on Good Friday, and to wear the clippings.

Stone the Toads

Pliny's *Natural History* tells readers that a magic toad's bone has many miraculous properties, including the ability to end quarrels and act as an aphrodisiac. This is probably the basis of the belief in toadstones. It wasn't easy to get one, so the effort involved had to be worth all of the trouble. Therefore, a toadstone was supposed to grant mastery over animals, people and witches, and prevent or mitigate pain during childbirth.

Belief in toadstones lasted from the sixteenth to the late eighteenth century. In fact, when toadstones were later examined, most were actually fossilized fish teeth.

The process started by putting a dead toad on an anthill, and waiting for the ants to clean the flesh from the bones. These were taken and thrown into running water. The one bone that floated was the toadstone.

The Font of Goodness

From the eighteenth century until the early twentieth century, the holy water kept in a church font was believed to be a powerful protector from ghosts and witchcraft. The belief was so powerful that fonts had to be kept locked, something still seen today. Until they were christened, babies were kept inside the house because they were thought to be extremely vulnerable to disease, the evil eye, or being stolen by witches or fairies, and only baptizing them could protect them.

Bathing your eyes with baptismal water would stop you from seeing ghosts.

The water also protected both children and adults from witchcraft, and stopped sleepwalking. It had to be poured over the nocturnal walker while they were awake, but it had to be unexpected and a shock for them.

Turned Clothes

In the nineteenth century in Yorkshire, England, young women regularly wore their clothes inside out, hoping to protect their husbands or boyfriends from danger while they were at sea.

Putting a piece of clothing on inside out accidentally has been said to bring both good and bad luck.

Silver Services

Silver is credited with many talismanic uses:

- Silver collected at church was thought to be blessed. For a charm against fits, you exchanged some for your own

coins, melted it down, and made a ring. Silver rings were also believed to help cramps.

- Cattle that were believed to be attacked by elves had water that previously contained a piece of silver poured over them.
- Bridegrooms would put something silver in the sole of their shoe to ward off fairies, who enjoyed the happiness of a wedding.
- A milkmaid may put a silver coin in the churn if cream would not turn to butter.

Eye to Eye

Having an evil eye cast upon you was blamed for many afflictions. The best way to counteract this was to have something that could outstare the evil eye. Because they appear to have a fixed stare, goats in Britain were kept with valuable cattle as living amulets. However, the blue eye beads of glass found throughout the Mediterranean are much better known. Designs vary tremendously but there is always a blue element and something like an eye—often just a few concentric circles. Historically, a stone called eye agate was used. This has natural layers of different shades of blue, and it was carved to show eye-like circles.

Holey Stones

For centuries stones with natural holes in them have been carried as amulets to provide protection from witches and fairies. Larger stones were hung in stables to prevent the horses from being hag-ridden; If a horse looked uncharacteristically

Holed stones were also hung in bedrooms to protect the sleeper from evil, particularly nightmares caused by creatures such as goblins sitting on your chest at night.

Shot by the Elves

Prehistoric arrowheads made from flint were believed to be the remnants of people who were driven into hiding, and had become elves or fairies. The arrowheads were worn as amulets to protect against being elf-shot (attacked by elves). Perhaps the elves would mistake you for an elf, and therefore not shoot you.

Animals reckoned to be afflicted by elf shot were cured by being touched with an ancient arrowhead, or by drinking water in which one had been dipped.

sweaty, tired, and nervous in the morning, it was believed that witches had stolen and ridden it to exhaustion during the night.

Hangman's Rope

In the seventeenth century, a piece of hangman's rope tied around your head was thought to cure a headache, and until the twentieth century it was believed to help epilepsy. There are no explanations for this superstition, but because the philosopher Pliny endorsed it, the notion was accepted without question by generation after generation.

Any Cold Iron

From the late eighteenth century to the mid-twentieth century, touching iron was a protective charm. This superstition most likely related to the idea that metal repels fairies and witches. Other associated beliefs include:

■ If a sailor used one of the words forbidden at sea or saw someone he thought to be a witch, he would touch iron or say "cold iron" as an antidote.

- Iron tools and horseshoes were kept or hung up in stables to protect horses from being hag-ridden.
- If a dairymaid's cream was not turning into butter, she often assumed that it had been cursed by a witch. A heated horseshoe dropped into the cream would remove the spell.

Animal Mascots

Shrew Me the Way

Shrews were once believed to be poisonous, and it was thought that they could make animals or humans lame just by crawling onto them. Anyone believing this in the sixteenth century would encase a live shrew in clay, allow it to dry, and hang the combination around the neck of the animal or person they wished to protect. In 1936 you could still find people who believed that carrying a dead shrew in their pocket prevented rheumatism.

Dogged Determination

Mascots are living animals that are thought to bring success simply by their presence. They tend to be popular with sports teams in particular. A well-known mascot in the late 1800s was Owney, a mongrel dog who wandered into the Albany, New York, post office in 1888. Because he was thin, cold, and blind in one eye, the staff decided to take him in.

One day he followed a mail wagon to the station, where he got on a train unnoticed and was transported out of town. He eventually came back on another train, but he caught the travel bug, and began taking trains to other places. He always came back to Albany, and so the post office workers gave him a collar and tag with his name and address on it.

When Owney visited a new post office, the clerks often added a tag of their own to show where he had been. When he returned to Albany, all but the original tag was taken off his collar and kept as souvenirs. He soon became associated with good luck because the trains were never in a wreck.

Owney journeyed in mail cars, and even on ocean steamers, to places as far away as Asia and Europe.

The Japanese mikado gave him a silver medal, inscribed with the Japanese coat of arms. But when Owney was in Toledo, Ohio, he was chained to a post in the post office while the staff waited for a photographer. Unused to such treatment, he bit the hand of one of the workers. The worker assumed Owney had gone mad and called a policeman, who shot Owney. The Albany postal workers were grief-stricken, and asked for the body to be returned.

Today Owney's stuffed body, and the collection of tags he amassed, are in a glass case in the U.S. Postal Museum in Washington, D.C.

Sharp Practices

A knife placed in a baby's cradle was believed to protect against evil influences—perhaps this was an extension of the witch- and fairy-repellent properties of iron. A knife with the blade facing up would be placed beneath the bed as a cure for epilepsy.

Numbers

Superstitions about numbers are among the most tenacious worldwide, perhaps because many of the events that shape human experiences are linked by the same numbers. In China and other Asian countries, a number is considered lucky or unlucky because of the sound of the word for it. In the West, it's more likely to come from an association with religion, nature, or history.

Don't Count on It...

We all have our own lucky numbers, too. Even if we don't really believe in the luck that they may or may not bring, we note when they appear in a house address, telephone number, or lottery ticket number. The numbers become lucky or unlucky tokens according to our experience.

Ignorance Is Bliss

Some superstitious people have a long-standing belief that the Fates are against them, and it is very bad luck to tempt them any further. Demonstrating too much confidence in the future might cause divine or supernatural retribution. The superstitious were often averse to counting, measuring, or weighing anything they valued, such as:

- Babies: Weighing or measuring babies was thought to tempt the Fates to do something horrible. In addition, the more knowledge that fairies, elves, and witches had of human affairs, the more likely they would interfere. It was even unlucky to count the stars.
- Livestock: "Don't count your chickens before they hatch!" is one of the best-known superstitions involving counting, or counting on good luck. Nervous fishermen also avoided counting their fish before they had landed them, shepherds wouldn't count their lambs until the lambing season was over, and bakers wouldn't count the cakes they had baked.
- Winnings: Gamblers notoriously refuse to count their winnings until they have finished playing. If you tempt the Fates by doing so, they might just ensure that the next turn of a card or spin of a wheel takes it all away.

217

However, counting was a good thing when part of a healing ritual. Typically, a wart sufferer would count their warts, collect the same number of small white stones from running water, and rub each wart with one of them. The stones would be wrapped in paper, tied up to make a parcel, and thrown over the left shoulder at the nearest crossroads. When someone eventually picked up the parcel, the warts would magically transfer to that person. Healers in the late nineteenth and early twentieth centuries claimed they could cure warts only by knowing the sufferer's name and the exact number of their warts.

In Britain it is unlucky to count the stones in ancient monuments such as Stonehenge.

Curiously it was also thought to be impossible to count the stones. King Charles II and writers Daniel Defoe, John Evelyn, and Celia Fiennes all ignored the superstition to add up the Stonehenge monoliths, and each ended up with a different tally.

Counting on the Future
Counting magpies is still believed to tell you what the future holds, which could be good or bad, according to the number you encounter.

Odds and Evens
Western superstition usually regards odd numbers as lucky and even ones as unlucky. Shakespeare mentioned this in *The Merry Wives of Windsor* in 1597, but it had been a common belief since classical times. In the United States, many people believe a two-dollar bill is unlucky, so they tear off the corners. This is said to remove any curse, perhaps because the torn-off corners are triangles—a potent and mystic three-sided shape.

The numbers three, five, seven, and nine are encountered frequently in cures and other traditions, but this may be simply because they are low numbers and are easy to count or collect.

The number four is trickier. As an even number it is unlucky, yet there are four elements—earth, air, fire, and water—and four major compass points. To complicate things even more, both the three-leaf shamrock of Ireland and the rarer four-leaf clover are lucky.

Special Numbers

Lucky, Lucky, Lucky

Odd numbers are generally luckier than even ones, and threes are often considered luckiest of all. Yet the number three has a reputation for both good and bad luck. Pythagoras thought three was the perfect number—the symbol of a beginning, middle, and end. Perhaps it is that simple. However, there are other theories about threes:

- It's commonly thought that bad luck comes in threes, and lighting three cigarettes from one match is said to be fatal.
- "Third time lucky!" is a common exhortation, hoping that after two tries a third will be successful. This might simply be a way to encourage others to try harder. "Third time prove best" appears in the poem "Sir Gawain and the Green Knight," from about 1375.
- Three candles burning on a table are said to predict a funeral, but some people believe it means there will be a wedding soon.
- Starting in the late 1800s, people believed a death in a community was a forewarning for another two.
- Some people believe if they break something, another two breaks will quickly follow. Therefore, they will deliberately break two things of little value to lessen the future damage.

Heavenly Triumvirates

The Holy Trinity of Father, Son, and Holy Spirit in Christianity is a core belief for Christians. And both the Old and New Testaments refer to other groups of three:

- St. Peter's three denials
- Three lions in Daniel's den
- Three days after which Jesus was said to have risen
- Three days Jonah spent in the whale

But the importance of trinities is not confined to Christianity. Classical Hinduism, which dates back to at least 500 B.C., has a divine Trinity. It is worshiped as one being rather than three: Brahma, the Father or supreme God; Vishnu, the incarnate Word and Creator; and Shiva, the Spirit of God. Islam has three main holy sites: Mecca, Medina, and Jerusalem.

Ancient Egyptians worshiped a trinity of the father, mother, and child, which made a family the most powerful symbol for the continuity of life. This trinity was often represented as a triangle. This may be why they built pyramids to bury their most illustrious citizens.

The academic year is divided into three semesters. The Earth is a trinity of land, sea, and air.

Struck Out

Lighting a third cigarette from the same match is a superstition that most likely began during the Boer War or World War I. It was a warning that by the time a third cigarette is lit, the match has been ignited long enough for the enemy to take aim and fire—killing the third smoker.

In Celtic tradition a young woman, a mother, and a crone represent the mother goddess. They also represented continuity through family. This always came down the maternal line, presumably because it is more difficult to establish paternity.

In Roman mythology, three gods ruled over the world, and each deity was usually depicted with a symbol based on three components:

- Jupiter ruled over heaven, and was pictured with a lightning streak made of three lines.
- Neptune was lord of the sea and carried a trident.
- Pluto's special dominion was Hades or Hell, which was guarded by the three-headed dog, Cerberus.

Minor deities also came in threes, including the three Fates, the three Graces, and the three Furies.

Four No More

The number four is considered unlucky by Chinese, Vietnamese, Korean, and Japanese people, because their term for it sounds like the word for death. Companies based in those countries that use serial numbers to identify products simply do not use the number four, and in some buildings there is no fourth floor.

666 and All That

This verse in the Book of Revelations is why so many people believe the number 666 represents the Devil:

And he causeth all, both small and great, rich and poor, free and bond, to receive a mark in their right hand, or in their foreheads. And that no man might buy or sell, save he that had the mark, or the name of the beast, or the number of his name. Here is wisdom. Let him that hath understanding count the number of the beast: for it is the number of a man: and his number is Six hundred threescore and six.

—The Bible, King James Version

Yet the passage is subject to many other interpretations. A widespread modern conspiracy theory suggests the number is secretly contained in the bar codes of all retail goods, and these will activate some terrible thing when the Devil is ready. The impending disaster has never been described, but trying to persuade a believer against this theory usually evokes the response that the doubter is actually part of the conspiracy.

The lucky thing about a number like 666 it that is doesn't occur in daily life as often as 13. But the perceived problem can persist up until death. When purchasing a grave site, some people have asked for a grave to be renumbered from 666 to another number.

Yet 666 is particularly lucky for the Chinese. The number 6 is one of their luckiest numbers because it sounds like the word for flowing or smooth, so it is taken to mean that life will go smoothly.

Therefore, in China, the number 666 is interpreted to have triple good luck.

Lucky 7

Seven has an almost universally positive place in superstitions. Astrologers once thought that seven planets controlled the universe and that the life of man was divided into seven ages—notably explained by Shakespeare in *As You Like It:*

All the world's a stage,
And all the men and women merely players:
They have their exits and their entrances;

And one man in his time plays many parts,
His acts being seven ages. At first the infant,
Mewling and puking in the nurse's arms.
And then the whining schoolboy, with his satchel,
And shining morning face, creeping like snail
Unwillingly to school. And then the lover,
sighing like furnace, with a woeful ballad
Made to his mistress' eyebrow. Then a soldier,
Full of strange oaths, and bearded like the pard,
Jealous in honour, sudden and quick in quarrel,
Seeking the bubble reputation
Even in the cannon's mouth. And then the justice,
In fair round belly with good capon lined,
With eyes severe, and beard of formal cut,
Full of wise saws and modern instances;
And so he plays his part. The sixth age shifts
Into the lean and slippered pantaloon,
With spectacles on nose and pouch on side,
His youthful hose well saved a world too wide
For his shrunk shank; and his big manly voice,
Turning again towards childish treble, pipes
And whistles in his sound. Last scene of all.
That ends this strange eventful history
Is second childishness, and mere oblivion,
Sans teeth, sans eyes, sans taste, sans everything.

- A seventh child, particularly a seventh son, was thought to have special healing powers and the ability to see ghosts.
- It is still commonly believed that our bodies and minds change over the course of seven years, so we encounter a significant change at the end of each cycle.
- The traditional coming of age at 21 is the end of three seven-year cycles.
- The 63rd year—7 times 9—of a person's life is sometimes believed to be one that brings great danger or ill health. If a person survives and lives to 64, they will go on to live a long life.

Mystic Multiplication

The number nine may be a mystical and lucky number because it is three times three. Since the number three is fortunate, three times three is considered to be even better.

Followers of Pythagoras, the ancient Greek mathematician, believed that man was the equivalent of eight notes of a full musical chord, and God was the completing ninth.

In classical mythology there are nine Muses, nine heads of the Hydra, and the nine circles in which the Styx flowed around Hell. In Scandinavian mythology there are nine worlds. The ninth world was a cold, dark wasteland ruled by Hel, and called Niflheim, which contained nine more worlds.

The Cantonese think the number nine is lucky, because in their dialect it sounds like the word for sufficient. However, nine is unlucky in most parts of China, simply because it is an odd number.

Premium Prices

In Chinese culture, the number eight is considered a very lucky number. The word for eight in both Mandarin and Cantonese sounds similar to the word for prosperity. In fact, 88 looks very much like the Chinese symbol for *shuang xi* or double joy. Homebuyers prefer the number eight. In fact some have their address and telephone number changed to include the number. A car license plate with one or more eights can sell for a premium of hundreds or thousands of dollars.

Clubbed Together

In New York in the 1880s, 13 men formed the Thirteen Club to show their scorn for the superstitions of the time. The charter meeting took place at 13 minutes past 8 on Friday, January 13, 1882, and lasted until the 13th hour, in Room 13 of Knickerbocker Cottage.

The members agreed to meet for dinner on the 13th day of every month. The fee for lifetime membership was $13, the initiation cost was $1.13, and monthly dues were 13 cents. The members spent their meetings scorning other superstitions—deliberately spilling salt and breaking mirrors.

By 1887 the club had over 400 members, and over time it had five American presidents as honorary members, including Chester Arthur, Grover Cleveland, Benjamin Harrison, William McKinley and Theodore Roosevelt. It was so successful that a sister club was formed in London.

Nest Eggs

The Roman writer Pliny, recorded the belief that an odd number of eggs in a nest was the best assurance of hatching plenty of hens rather than unproductive rooster chicks. From the late nineteenth century onward it was believed that the ideal number was 13 eggs. Yet at the same time in history the number 13 was becoming unlucky in popular belief.

Sporting Fixtures

Athletes are notoriously superstitious, though many teams have someone wearing a number 13 shirt. While it was unlucky for some, it certainly wasn't for others.

In the October playoffs, Branca pitched the ball for New York Giants Bobby Thomson's "shot heard around the world" home run—one of the most famous home runs of all time. The Dodgers lost 5–4 to the Giants, and the pitch now holds a memorable place in baseball history.

In basketball, Wilt Chamberlain said his number 13 shirt was unlucky only for his opponents. And he was certainly one of the greatest players of the game. He was the only National

Baseball player Ralph Branca laughed off superstition and wore the number 13 shirt when pitching for the Brooklyn Dodgers —he even posed for a photograph while holding a black cat.

Basketball Association player to score 4000 points in a season, and during the 1961–62 season he averaged 50.4 points per game. He also set records for most points in a game, most consecutive field goals, and the most rebounds. The number 13 didn't seem to bring bad luck for Chamberlain.

Freaky Friday

The bad luck associated with Friday the thirteenth is one of the most famous superstitions. From the seventeenth century

Nine Lives

Cats are rumored to have nine lives because they seem to survive when they are taking great risks, such as leaping or falling from great heights. But in the sixteenth century it was believed that this happened because a witch could inhabitat the body of a cat nine times.

However, the origins of this superstition could go back as far as ancient Egypt. The priesthood of Heliopolis worshiped Atum-Ra, a sun god. Atum-Ra gave life to four gods of the earth, air, water, and sky. They in turn produce Osiris, Isis, Seth, and Nephthys. The two groups of four plus Atum-Ra formed the Ennead, or the Nine, and Atum-Ra embodied all nine lives. When he visited the underworld, he was believed to take the form of a cat.

onward, enormous numbers of almanacs were printed and eagerly read. Their objective was to provide information about dates that were lucky or unlucky for readers. Friday the thirteenth was never singled out. A tragic event falling on Friday the thirteenth is not mentioned in any of the tragedies and ominous events dramatized by the playwrights of the sixteenth and seventeenth centuries, and contemporary books on superstition in the late nineteenth and early twentieth centuries do not mention Friday the thirteenth as unlucky, either.

In 1891, the American publication *Belford's Magazine* printed an article titled "The Thirteen Superstition among the Fair Sex," containing letters from well-known American women. They all refer to the bad luck of 13 at the table, but none of them mention it in connection with a Friday.

Fridays have been considered unlucky only since the Middle Ages, and the connection with the number 13 goes back only to Victorian times.

A Cat for Luck

At London's Savoy Hotel, a sculpture of Kaspar the cat is brought out whenever 13 dinner guests are expected. Wearing a napkin around its neck and served every course, it makes the fourteenth guest.

This tradition has its origins in 1898 when Wolf Joel, a South African guest at the Savoy, held a dinner party for 13, in defiance of the superstition. Not long after his return to South Africa, Joel was shot and killed. After the hotel heard the news, a staff member was required to attend any dinner party with 13 guests. In 1926 Kaspar was created to do the job instead.

Going Up?

Fourteen is considered the unluckiest number in Chinese culture because its pronunciation sounds like the phrase for guaranteed death. Many hotels omit this floor in their numbering system, and because of the West's distrust of 13, some go directly from the twelfth to the fifteenth floor.

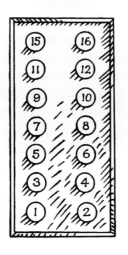

Unluckiest—or Not?

The perception of the number 13 as unlucky is so widespread among English-speaking cultures that most people think it is a very ancient superstition. Yet the earliest reference to 13 as a generally unlucky number dates back to 1852—and this was for the idea that it was unlucky to have 13 people at a table or in company.

By the late eighteenth century it was a common belief that the first person to rise from a table of 13 would be the next to die. To negate this fate, everyone would rise from the table at the same time, presumably confusing the Fates. Or some people would be seated at another table to avoid having 13 in one place.

To this day, houses with a 13 in the address don not sell as well as other numbers. Some builders skip the number or use 12a instead. Apartment buildings and hotels frequently lack a thirteenth floor, and sometimes stable blocks omit the number.

One prevailing theory about the roots of the unlucky 13 superstition comes from the sixteenth and seventeenth centuries, when it was believed that witches' covens had 13 members. However, there is little hard evidence of covens ever existing, and any available "proof" there is does not mention 13 as significant. The idea of witches meeting in covens of 13 was repopularized by the British anthropologist Margaret Alice Murray in the 1920s. But she also had scant evidence for the practice and seems to have distorted the evidence about most 13-member covens she lists.

A second theory is based in mythology, where Odin, chief of the Norse gods, held a banquet in Valhalla for 12 people. But Loki the trickster giant arrived, making the number 13. He then murdered the god Balder or Balduro.

However, according to the original poem, Lokasenna, the banquet was held by Aegir, not Odin, and the number of guests was 18—including Loki—and the murder of Balder did not take place in Valhalla!

A third, and currently most dominant, theory is based on the number of guests at the Last Supper of Jesus and his disciples.

Even before Henry VIII's Reformation of the Catholic Church in England and the establishment of the Anglican Church, many clergy and worshipers felt they owed greater allegiance to their monarch than to the pope. So they often made a point of living closely to the ways Jesus lived. This included gathering in groups of 13, just like the Last Supper.

However, after the Reformation, the new Protestant church said these copycat activities were superstitious, and they were forbidden. Meeting in groups of 13 took on a bad connotation. This means that general bad luck was associated with the number since the late sixteenth century, but it became a popular superstition rather recently.

It is also possible that 13 is regarded as unlucky simply because it is one number beyond 12. Twelve—said to be the number of perfection—is seen in the 12 months of a year, 12 hours in a day, and 12 signs of the zodiac.

Calendar Customs & Rituals

Many calendar customs, including rites originally related to crop planting or harvest, have taken on a significance over and above the practical, which brings them into the realm of superstition. Cornhusk dolls, for example, may be seen by some as no more than a celebration of harvest time, but for others they have come to be symbolic of fertility in general. The beginning of a new year is, perhaps, the most significant of all calendar customs, representing a new start. It is celebrated on different dates in different cultures, and in many different ways.

New Year, Old Beliefs

The start of a new year is usually an important holiday that is celebrated in almost every culture around the world. A new beginning is a chance for a fresh start. According to superstitious people, however, this is only possible if you say or do the right thing. It doesn't seem to make a difference that the Chinese, Jews, and other groups have different New Year's Days from the rest of the world, or that the start of spring can be judged by a calendar date, a blossom, or an animal activity. Wherever you celebrate, the New Year is particularly significant because it a harbinger of what is in store for the next 12 months.

Will the Real New Year's Day Please Stand Up?

Historically, important dates such as New Year's Day could fall on different dates. Scotland officially adopted January 1 at the beginning of 1600, but England, Ireland, and Wales resisted this until 1752. For these countries, the official and religious New Year began on March 25—but there were those who disagreed. For example, in 1666 the London writer Samuel Pepys marked January 1 in his London diary as New Year's Day.

Rituals for a Happy New Year

Certain actions were believed to influence the type of luck and level of prosperity you would have in the year to come. These rituals took place at midnight on New Year's Eve or New Year's Day. Some traditions included:

- Superstitious people went to amazing lengths to be sure that something came into the house before something left it on New Year's Day. Some people kept a log fire or

a candle burning during New Year's Eve until the following morning, believing that this would ensure that the household had heat, light, and cooking fuel all year long. But it was important that none of that fire left the house. In fact, there was a general warning of bad luck if any objects left the house on New Year's Day. And because they were such staples, salt and fire were the possessions that people worried about the most.

- To guarantee that money flowed into the house, and not out, a coin was tied to a piece of string and placed outside the door or a window before midnight on New Year's Eve. Once the clock struck 12, the string was drawn back into the house to retrieve the coin. This way, not even the homeowner's hand went out of the house before the coin came in.

- When midnight strikes, some superstitious people get up, stand up, or go upstairs before they go down, sit down, or walk downstairs. This action ensures that things are going to be positive and upwardly mobile throughout the coming year. In the Philippines, children jump up and down at midnight on New Year's Eve to make sure they grow tall.

- Some people leave all of their windows and doors open to "let in the New Year and chase out the old," hoping to encourage money to come in with the New Year.

- It was believed that the girl who drew the first bucket of water from a well on New Year's Day would be happy and find love. However, doing the laundry on that day would cause a death in the family.

When to Hang a Calendar

Some people believe there are some days throughout the year that are luckier, or unluckier, than others. But you could only take advantage of the lucky days if you hung your new calendar up on New Year's Day. If you hung it up before then, you could expect 365 days of rotten luck.

First Footing

"First footing" on New Year's Day originated in the British Isles around the middle of the nineteenth century, and it is traditionally thought of as a particularly Scottish tradition. There are some early references to Christmas Day first footings, but these date only from the beginning of the nineteenth century. Some first footing superstitions are:

- If the first person to set foot in your house on New Year's Day had positive personal characteristics, it was very good luck. Desiring tall, dark men as first-footers is a fairly recent trend. In Scotland a fair- or red-haired man was once thought to bring maximum luck. A woman first-footer was almost universally thought unlucky, presumably because men were more likely to cross the threshold with money or food during the coming year.
- First-footers brought symbolic gifts with them; these were usually a staple of life, such as food, drink, heat, or light.
- Symbolic actions that first-footers took to increase the luck of the household included cutting a cake, visiting every room in the house, and almost invariably, wishing everyone a Happy New Year.
- If the first-footer stumbled when entering a house, he himself could have ill luck in the coming year. "Breaking" a cake by cutting it in a messy fashion, or shattering the plate on which it was served, meant very bad luck for the household.

Bible Dipping

Predicting your future with the Bible was another New Year's Day ritual. The family bible was placed on a table before breakfast, and anyone who wished to know what would happen to them in the coming year opened it at random and placed their index finger on a page. Others in the room would read the selected text, and attempt to interpret it in light of the individual's circumstances. Dipping also happened at other times during the year, such as at the start of a journey or any

new endeavor. But it was, and still is in some families, primarily a New Year custom.

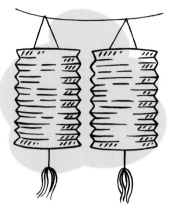

Chinese New Year
The Chinese New Year occurs around the northern winter solstice, when there are the fewest hours of daylight, so the actual date varies from year to year. The celebrations last for several days and end with paper lanterns hung everywhere, along with a grand procession lead by the famous Lion Dancers. However, the house must be cleaned before New Year's Day, and all cleaning equipment should be put away on New Year's Eve. For superstitious people, sweeping on New Year's Day meant sweeping away good fortune. For continued good luck after New Year's Day, dust is swept from the doorway to the middle of the room and stored in corners. The dust must stay there until the fifth day and no one must step on the dust piles.

A bright and happy shade of red is usually seen and worn during Chinese New Year celebrations.

Lights Out
The end of the Christmas period was once held on Candlemas, or February 2. This festival celebrates the Virgin Mary's purification and the presentation of the infant Jesus at the temple, 40 days after his birth. Candles were sprinkled with holy water and blessed. Sometimes the ends of these candles were sewn into clothing and worn to keep away evil spirits. As at New Year, it was considered lucky to bring items into the house before letting anything out of the house on Candlemas.

This follows the belief that a person who looks and feels happy on that day will feel that way for the whole year. Children and unmarried young people are given little red envelopes containing money. These are believed to protect them from evil spirits, and bring them health and wealth during the new year.

Chinese New Year Etiquette
When celebrating Chinese New Year:

- Look to the future rather than back over the past year.
- Make no reference to dead friends or relatives.
- Do not cry on New Year's Day or you will be crying all year. Children who misbehave are tolerated much more at this time. It's likely they will be not shouted at or disciplined in order to prevent them from crying.

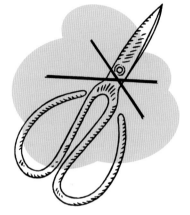

Do not use knives or scissors at Chinese New Year because they might cut off good fortune.

A Date for Love

The Love of Valentine
The original St. Valentine was possibly a rebel priest in ancient Rome, who was executed on February 14 in A.D. 270 because he believed in love and marriage. The emperor Claudius was having trouble in recruiting soldiers, and he thought it was because men preferred to stay at home with their wives and children. Therefore, he banned marriage. This was mostly ignored and St. Valentine willingly performed marriage ceremonies in secret until he was arrested and thrown into

Let me
be your Valentine

jail. Augustine, the jailer's daughter, was kind to Valentine, so he sent her a note signed "from your Valentine," as many cards are signed today.

Heart's Content

Valentine's Day has been celebrated in one way or another since at least the fourteenth century. At that time, groups of single men or women would draw names from a hat to find their valentine for the year. Sometimes men pinned the piece of paper with their Valentine's name on their sleeve for a week. This might be the origin of the saying "to wear your heart on your sleeve."

Even if you were not attracted to the person whose name you had drawn, the custom was to be friendly and exchange letters and small gifts over the course of the year. And sometimes this would end in love and romance, which gave hope to everyone else.

The best and luckiest thing that could happen to you was to be woken with a kiss on St. Valentine's Day.

Flying Foresight

If a woman was determined to get a preview of her spouse, she could visit a graveyard at midnight on St. Valentine's Eve, and run around the church 12 times chanting any special charms she knew. She would then see his face if she slept with a sprig of rosemary under her pillow. Or on Valentine's Day a woman could keep her eyes on the skies. The first animal she saw flying overhead would tell her more about the man she might marry:

- A robin meant she would marry a sailor or crime fighter.
- A sparrow meant a happy marriage to a poor man.
- A goldfinch meant she'd marry a rich man.

- A bat meant she would marry a baseball player.
- A flock of doves signified a happy, peaceful marriage.

But there were telling signs in other places:

- Seeing a squirrel meant the man she would marry would hoard all of their money.
- Finding a man's glove was exciting because the man with the other one would be her spouse.

If all of the superstitions she knew had not worked, a young hopeful could always drop a handkerchief or glove in the path of an attractive man, hoping he would pick it up and notice her.

A Rose Is a Rose

Because it is undeniably the flower of love, the rose is the blossom most people choose to give to their beloved on Valentine's Day. A rosebud stands for beauty, youth, and an innocent heart, and a single red rosebud represents purity and loveliness. Both a single red rose in full bloom and a dozen red roses mean love.

Many traditions associate different shades of roses with particular emotions. Unfortunately, several colors have been given more than one meaning, so their messages may be unclear.

Adam's Apple

A man seeking knowledge of his future bride on Valentine's Day could recite a list of potential spouses while twisting the stem of an apple. When the apple fell from the broken stem, the name he had been reciting at the time would belong to his sweetheart.

Some generally accepted meanings for roses are:

- Coral: desire
- Lavender: enchantment and individuality
- Orange: fascination
- Peach: modesty, gratitude, admiration, and sympathy
- Pale pink: grace, joy, and happiness
- Dark pink: friendship and admiration
- Red: love, respect, and courage
- Deep red: beauty and passion
- White: innocence, purity, reverence, and humility
- Yellow: friendship, joy, jealousy, freedom, and hope

A flower associated with Valentine's Day is the violet, considered to be the symbol of fidelity. It is believed that violets grew outside the cell where St. Valentine was imprisoned.

Is Spring Sprung?

Hogging the Light

For as the sun shines on Candlemas Day,
so far will the snow swirl in May.

This ancient superstition is the basis for Groundhog Day on February 2nd in the United States and Canada. When a groundhog—also known as a marmot or a woodchuck—pops his head out of his burrow on that day, it means one of two things, both of which seem to be the opposite of what you'd expect:

- If it is cloudy and he cannot see his shadow on the ground, he knows it will soon be spring, and he stays outside.
- If it is sunny and he sees his shadow, he returns to the burrow and sleeps for six more weeks, which is how much longer the winter will last.

The tradition is so popular that groundhogs that have predicted the weather reliably are named after the place they live. Punxsutawney Phil in Pennsylvania and Holtsville Hal in New York State are just two that receive a lot of public attention.

The New World's groundhog could have solved a lot of arguments in the Old World. Celtic countries thought that spring began with the festival of Imbolc at the beginning of February. But others thought it began six weeks later with the vernal equinox in late March, when there were at last more daylight hours than dark ones.

Washing your face in May dew was supposed to be good for your complexion. And it was believed to stop your face from tanning in the sun and to prevent freckles.

Cuckoo Years

Hearing the first cuckoo was commonly believed to mark the coming of spring in Britain and Europe. And what you were doing when you heard the bird was thought to predict the year ahead for you:

- If you had money in your pocket, you would have money all year, especially if you immediately turned it over in your wallet or pocket.
- If you were in bed, it meant you'd be sick or die before the season or the year was out.

- If you were hungry, you would be hungry another year.
- If you were standing somewhere hard, you'd be hard up or have a hard time.
- If you were idle, you'd be idle for a year.

You could counteract the predictions by spitting or by taking positive action. To make up for being idle, for example, you could run quickly in a circle, or roll on the ground. If that was too much effort, you could ask your friends to roll you.

Casting Doubts

There are two explanations for the popular English superstition that goes with the saying, "Ne'er cast a clout till May is out." A clout was an extra protective layer worn during winter. So for some this meant you shouldn't remove a clout until the hawthorn or may trees were in bloom. For most people, it was a warning to stay wrapped up until the month of May ended. In fact, in Britain in the early 1700s. the saying was applied as a general warning against hasty actions of any kind. But there's an earlier 1627 Spanish proverb, which says the same thing: "Hasta Mayo no te quites el sano."

Maidens washing in the dew of the first day of May could make a wish.

Midsummer Coal

It was once believed that on Midsummer's Eve or Day (June 23), coal could be found buried beneath plantain or mugwort plants. If you found a piece of coal, it kept your house safe from plague, lightning, fevers, and fire. In the late 1600s young girls eagerly sought this magical talisman, believing that placing a piece under their pillows meant they would dream of their future husbands.

Easter Dressing

Although Good Friday and Easter Sunday could be as early as March in some years, they were both popular days to begin wearing fewer clothes. But whenever you did it, Sunday was considered the best day because superstitious people believed prayers that were said would save you from catching a cold.

Easter was also the time to wear new clothes to ward off ill luck. The practice goes back to at least since the sixteenth century, but it invited bad luck if you wore something new before Easter. In Shakespeare's play *Romeo and Juliet* Mercutio asks, "Didst thou not fall out with a tailor for wearing his new doublet before Easter?"

May kittens were believed to be unlucky, no good at catching mice, and liable to bring snakes into the house. It was once common to drown kittens born in May.

Defining Days

Freed Spirits

Many cultures have a special day of festivities to celebrate the spirits of the dead. The Mexican Day of the Dead, now marked on November 1 and 2, is one of these. However, before the Spanish introduced Roman Catholicism to Mexico, the celebration was held during the summer.

Elsewhere, Halloween, an abbreviation of All Hallows Eve, falls on October 31. Because so many spirits were believed to be roaming free on Halloween, it was a good time for divinations of love or death. For instance, individually marked ivy leaves were left in a bowl overnight, and people expected

Irish Spirits

Pre-Christian Ireland celebrated four main festivals, or quarter days: Imbolc in February, Beltane in May, Lughnasadh in August, and Samhain in November. This last one was the most important for tribal gatherings and feasts. And much like Halloween, there was a feeling that the physical and supernatural worlds were close and magical things could happen at this time of year. On that day the spirits of the dead and other supernatural entities were believed to pass into the world of humans. It was also a time to celebrate the end of the harvest, take stock of the herds, and store enough meat and grain for everyone to survive through the winter months. Often a communal bonfire was lit, and all other fires were put out. Then each family took fire from the bonfire and used it to light their own again, forming a symbolic bond between them.

to die in the following year would see a coffin shape on the leaf they had marked as their own.

The origin of the Halloween jack-o'-lantern comes from the story of a wicked man named Jack that God would not let into heaven. The man had also tricked the Devil into promising not to take his soul, so his spirit was condemned to walk the Earth forever. When the man asked the Devil how he would see without any light, he was thrown an ember from hell that would never go out. Jack carved out a turnip and put the ember in it for a lantern. Over time, pumpkins and squash for lanterns also became part of the tradition.

Today's—mostly North American—tradition of children visiting door to door and shouting out "trick or treat!" is based on the very ancient practice of going from door to door asking for food in return for prayers for the dead, known as souling. It has only been since the 1930s that the emphasis of Halloween has shifted from offering prayers to asking for candy.

Dismal Egyptians

The creators of almanacs and calendars used to mark certain days as *dies mala*—Latin for *bad days*—and the origin of our word *dismal*. They were also called cross or Egyptian days, because some people believed that calculating them went back to the time of ancient Egypt.

Bedroom Manners

In the days before spring mattresses, feather beds needed to be turned and plumped up every day. However, there was a common superstition that this should not be done on a Friday, and some people avoided Sundays, too.

This was good news to the poor housemaids who were charged with turning such heavy, unwieldy objects—usually found only in the richest houses. Turning a feather bed on a proscribed day was believed to make you unlucky in love. But the importance of a bed in so many major events from birth to death also generated predictions of illness, nightmares, or even death for the person who slept next in the bed.

Nightmares could be negated or banished if pillowcases were placed with their open ends facing out from the bed so that the nightmares had an easy way out.

Chamber Duties

Just getting out of bed improperly could affect a superstitious person's day. The idea that there is a right way and a wrong way to get up goes back at least to the sixteenth century, although instructions on achieving this ranged widely. In most early versions, you simply needed to get out of the right side

rather than the left. Some people thought it was more important to leave the bed on the same side you entered. Still others said you had to put your right foot on the floor before your left. And yet another bedroom superstition said make sure your bed was made before you left the room in the morning, or your next night's sleep would be disturbed.

Friday Feelings

Because Friday was the day of Christ's crucifixion, it has been associated with superstitious bad luck since at least the fourteenth century. The medieval church across Europe promoted Friday as a day of abstinence and penance in commemoration of the event—even being born on a Friday could bring bad luck for a child. In general, Friday was believed to be quite the wrong day to start a journey, get married, go fishing, or move to a new house.

Sundays are a close second. Both days were considered unlucky for cutting hair or nails, except Good Friday. This was considered a lucky day to cut your nails, as long as you had avoided all other Fridays.

Ausonios, a Latin poet, believed the safest days for grooming were: Tuesdays to cut nails, Wednesdays to trim your beard, and Friday to cut your hair.

Good Friday Exceptions

Blacksmiths were urged not to work on Good Friday. But if they—or anyone else—planted parsley on Good Friday, it would come up in double the planned amount. If you baked on a Friday, your house might burn down by the end of the year. However, bread baked on Good Friday was believed to have both lucky and magical properties: It supposedly never went stale or spoiled, remained edible for up to a year, and could be used in a number of cures.

Hung up or kept in a bag in the kitchen, Good Friday bread was said to protect against fires—especially those caused by baking on other Fridays—and, in some places, it was believed to guard against shipwrecks. Unsurprisingly, Good Friday bread also brought general good luck in the coming year. These superstitions supposedly originated from the story of a woman who gave Jesus a loaf of bread as he carried his cross to Gethsemane, and he blessed her for it.

Sunday Bests

It was bad luck—or sinful at least—to work on Sundays. However, new clothes were to be worn first on a Sunday, because they would then be blessed and last much longer.

Babies were dressed in their first toddler clothes on a Sunday.

To Wash or Not to Wash?

Superstitious people used to say that if you washed sheets on Holy Thursday or Ascension Day, you would be laid out on the same sheets before the next Holy Thursday. Good Friday and New Year's Day were also bad days for doing the laundry.

From about the middle of the nineteenth century onward, the day you did your laundry could bring you good or bad luck, as the following rhyme implies:

They who wash on Monday have all the week to dry
They who wash on Tuesday are not so much awry
They who wash on Wednesday are not so bad as the morrow
They who wash on Thursday wash for sorrow
They who wash on Friday wash in haste and need
They who wash on Saturday, oh, they are very bad indeed!

Holiday Customs

Lucky Christmas

Some people believe that following a holiday custom out of its rightful season—even if just a day early or late—would bring bad luck. At a time when Christmas decorations were mostly greenery, it was very unlucky to bring evergreen plants into the house before Christmas Eve. If you chose holly, it was important to bring in both smooth and prickly types to ensure a good coming year. If the prickly kind came in first, the master would rule the household for the year. However, if the smooth type entered the house first, his wife would be the dominant partner.

Disposing of the Christmas decorations also caused anxiety and superstitions. Some of the greenery was kept until Shrove Tuesday and then burned, ideally in a fire used to cook pancakes. Others thought burning them was sinful, and they would feed them to the cattle.

Christmas Logic

The Yule fire had to be set with enough wood to keep it burning all through Christmas Eve, but still have some logs untouched by the fire next morning. One of these pieces was kept for lighting the fire the following Christmas Eve.

It was believed to protect the house from fire throughout the year, so it was hung in the kitchen or placed somewhere else that needed protection. Sometimes it would be kept in the cowshed to shield the family cattle from hurt or mischief. The Yule log was a more difficult superstition to get right, because the same log was supposed to burn nonstop for the 12 days of Christmas.

Happy Pairs

Christmas Eve was one of the best times of the year for love divinations: If a girl walked backward to a pear tree and then circled it three times, she would see the spirit of her future husband. The other ideal times for love divinations were Valentine's Eve, Midsummer, and Halloween.

Cutting and Stirring Times

Although Christmas once ended at Candlemas (February 2), it is now usually taken to be January 6, or Twelfth Night. The number 12 also has other Christmas associations. For example, eating one mince pie in 12 different houses during the 12 days of Christmas brought good luck for the following 12 months. The first mince pie you ate was extra lucky; if you made a wish as you took your first bite, it would come true. Eating mince pies outside the 12 days of Christmas was very unlucky. And you never cut a mince pie or you would cut your luck.

It is a widespread tradition for each member of the family to stir the Christmas pudding mixture and to make a wish. If the wish is kept secret, it is supposed to come true.

If the Christmas pudding split when cooking or when put onto a plate, it meant one of the heads of the household would soon die.

Holy Innocents' Day

On December 28, Christians remember the night all first-born male children were massacred by King Herod in his vain attempt to avoid the rise of the new king, of whom he had been warned. Also known as Childermas Day, it is a grave and solemn day, even though it falls in the middle of the Christmas season. It was considered very unlucky to do laundry on that day. Superstitious people would not usually begin a new venture of any kind on Childermas. Very superstitious people believed that whatever day of the week it fell on would also be unlucky for the rest of the year.

Index

A

acorns
  carrying or wearing
    39, 191, 201
  placed on window ledge 201
  placing before a fire 67
  preserve youth and life 201
alabaster
  as cure for rabies 43
  ointment 42–3
amber 39, 188
amulets
  animal mascots 214–15
  arrowhead 213
  blue bead 203–4
  clothes as 211
  crosses 209
  garlic 207
  gold coin 209
  iron 213–14
  Islamic 201
  mole's paw 210
  plant 201
  pomanders 207
  red thread *see* red thread
  rope, hangman's 213
  silver 211–12
  spider 205
  stones as 212–13
  toadstones 210–11
  to ward off evil eye 35, 212
  to ward off evil spirits 147
  worn by mother and baby to
    keep evil spirits away 112
Angelica 147
apples
  fertility rituals 89
  peel thrown over shoulder
    9, 54

  twisting the stem of an 237
  used to divine future
    lover/spouse 9, 54, 237
April 113, 206
apron, untied 67
arrowheads 213
Ascension Day 14, 17, 245
ash twig 53
ax 22

B

babies
  appearance 106–7
  bathed in salt water 100–1
  birth days 103–4, 105, 108
  birthmarks 106
  boy or girl 99–100
  cats and 38
  clothes 100, 102
  cradles *see* cradles and cribs
  mirrors and 110
  nails and hair 108
  names 105
  predicting sex of 99–100
  pregnancy 94–7
  stepping over head of 102
  stones and 110
  teeth 108–10
  tickling feet of 99
  see also fertility
bats
  flying into house 27
  seeing on Valentine's Day
    73, 237
bear, riding a 40
bed
  an onion cut in half and
    placed under 37
  getting out of 28, 29, 243–4

  making or turning a
    20, 37, 69, 106, 243
  orientation of 37
bees
  flying into house 30, 173
  landing on head or hands
    12, 167
  landing on ship 174
  selling or giving away a hive
    125
  soul and 134
beetles 167–8
bells, ringing 50, 83, 151
Bible 233–4
birds
  appearing at window
    or entering house 169
  as cause of sickness 33
  as omens 27–8, 169
  droppings 169
  finding dead 169
  keeping eggs of in the house
    169
  souls and 134–5
  see also under individual
    bird name
blue beads 203–4, 212
bones 191
brambles 44
bread

association with death 50
baked on Good Friday 19, 245
baking to keep away fairies
    151
breaking in oven 182
bringing into a new house 14
burning 182
dropping 182
finding a hollow loaf 99
five loaves stuck together 182
four loaves stuck together 182
keep around a baby's neck 110
rising 64, 182
rubbing on warts 34
sin eating 141
slicing 182–3
two loaves stuck together 38
brides
    bouquets 85
    carrying over the threshold
        15, 86
    crossing a pig, hare or lizard 73
    crying on wedding day 83
    dress 79, 82
    mirrors and 23, 81
    rice throwing and 86, 95
    shoes 81, 84
    stocking throwing 85
    veil wearing 79
broom
    bringing into a new house 14
    leaping over 96
    passing over a single
        woman's feet 60
    sweeping out door with
        after dark 21
butterflies 137

C
cactus, planting a 27
cake
    blowing out candles on a 113

cutting a 233
    wedding 71
calendars
    hanging before the new year
        119
    hanging up on New Year's Day
        232
    see also under individual day
Candlemas 19, 234, 247
candles
    blowing or snuffing out
        113, 183
    corpse 145
    cutting in two 183
    dreaming of a black 50
    dripping on one side 183
    kept burning during
        New Year's Eve 232
    spotting a spark on 183–4
    three burning on a table 184
    to divine future love 60
    to ward off evil spirits
        8, 147
    "winding sheet" 50
caterpillar 168
cats
    and the dead 135
    astral travel 135, 136
    at the meeting point of
        five roads 118
    black cat
        29, 30, 117, 118, 122
    blood 38
    born in May 169
    buttering paws of 16
    death of 171
    deserting a house 30
    dreaming of 117, 171
    entering a room containing
        a dead body 30
    jumping over a body 135
    kissing a 29

laying on bed of a sick person
    30
Maneki Neko 118, 193
May kittens 241
meeting while walking with
    your love 71
nine lives of 226
on top of a tombstone 135
passing over a person 38
putting into a new house 16
sitting with its back to the fire
    30
sneezing 29–30, 72, 117, 171
splitting and binding round
    a knee 38
stroking a stye with tail of 38
theater 118, 130
    unusually playful activity in
        a 171
washing its face and paws 22
white 117, 171
chairs
    creaking 183
    gamblers turn 183
    knocking over 183
    turning while speaking 183
charms, good luck see under
    individual charm
chestnuts 66
chewing gum 130
chili peppers 189
Christmas 31, 54, 55, 56, 57,
    58, 59, 72, 90, 92, 104, 147,
    159, 207, 246–7
Christmas Day
    54, 72, 92, 147, 159, 247
Christmas Eve 55, 56, 57, 58,
    59, 104, 246, 247
circles 139
clocks
    falling, stopping, or chiming
        the wrong number 24

striking in a church 50
clothes
 dressing babies in old clothes
  or clothes for the opposite
  sex 100
 giving away all of babies' 102
 knitting for baby 102
 money in brings luck 123
 skirt catching in a doorway
  179
 skirt hem or jacket hem
  turned up 173
 wearing inside-out
  151, 179, 211
 wearing mourning clothes
  179, 181
clover
 four-leaf 187
 planting 151
 protecting your home with 7
 three-leaf 187
 two-leaf 53
coal
 as a gift 15
 as a good luck symbol 194
 bringing into a new house 14
 finding 240
cock crows
 if a girl hears 74
 in the afternoon 169
 predicts a visitor 21, 173
cockerels
 feeding pancakes to 69
 killing and burying 43
coins
 as gifts 15
 carrying for good luck
  121, 122–3
 finding 119, 120–1, 189
 gold 209
 New Year's Eve 232
 silver 212

colors 77
confetti 87
cork 46
cows
 donkey or goat kept in
  field with 90
 giving to the poor 136
 red thread tied around 35
cradles and cribs
 bringing into home 24
 buying 112
 knife placed in 112
 paying for 112
 rocking empty 113
crickets
 chirping or leaving house
  167
 in the kitchen 167
 killing 167
crosses 197, 198, 209
cross-eyed people 122
crossroads
 couples must avoid 71
 standing at 39
crows 122, 169
cuckoos 19, 50, 63, 68, 116,
  168, 239, 240
cutlery 22
daisy petals 9, 67
dandelions
 blowing off seeds 69
 tea to cure illness 39

D
Day of the Dead, Mexico
 133, 146, 241
death
 omens of 49–51
 touching corpse of 142
 destiny, controlling your 7–8
dogs
 and the dead 135

howling at night 8, 135, 171
 jumping over a body 135
 running between newly
  married couple 87
donkeys, child passed under
 and over 44
doors
 leaving open 232
 opening 143
 rehanging 145
doves 237
dragon's blood 66
dumb cake 59

E
Easter Sunday 241
eclipse 107
elder
 planting 16–17
 protective benefits 15
 to cure illness 39
eggs
 carrying into a house 22
 dreaming about rotten 181
 hung in roof of house 14
 ideal number of 90
 laid on Good Friday 19
 odd number of 225
 pouring white into water 63–4
 throw shells onto fire 125
 use in fertility rituals 96
eve agate 212
eyes
 itchy right eye 176
 itchy left eye 176
 left eye twitching 119
 right eye twitching 119

F
face painting 112
fairies
 calling their true name 150

horseshoes and 151
seeing 150
fasting 61
February 97
feet
babies born feet first 107–8
webbed toes 108
fennel 18
fertility
apples and 89
eggs and 96
fields and 95
Lupercalia and 96
maypole and 94–5
mistletoe and 92–3
moon and 91
number 13 and 90
nuts and 90, 93
plants and 94
sitting and 96
trees and 89–90
see also babies
fern 201
fingers
crooked 178
crossing 139
extra 178
folding your thumb inside 139
fire
cinders bouncing out of
99, 125
finding soot hanging from
the fire grate 22
holding a pinch of ash from
204
lighting 145
placing three bowls in front of
62
striking another person's 25–6
two people making up 26
see also hearth
fish

dreaming of
117, 118, 122, 125, 127
pouring wine down throat of
127
throwing back 126
flies 167
flowers 31
forge water 45
frankincense 147
frogs 40

G
gardens 95
garlic
hang over doorway 16, 145
medicinal use 207
planting 16
protects against vampires
207
garters 67, 68
geese 168
glass 84
glove 236
goats 212
goldfinch 236
Good Friday 100, 210, 241,
244–5
Groundhog Day 238–9

H
hair
divining color of 62–3
making a sandwich of 38
Halloween 31, 55, 56–7, 59,
62, 64, 104, 113, 136, 146,
147, 152, 153, 241–3
hands
baseball players spit into 130
dead man's 48
Fatima's 195, 197
washing with another person
26

hare
actors use foot 192
as bad luck 122, 191
feet as charms 192
meeting as unlucky 106, 192
meeting while pregnant
106, 192
running through town
or village 182
saying "hares" 198
hat 62
hawthorn 17
hazel 17
health and sickness
beds and 37
birds and 33
cats and 38
cures 37–49, 51
death, omens of 49–51
dogs and 42
evil eye and 34–5
herbs and 39
preventing illness 36
red thread and 35
rhyming for health 36
transference 44
warts 34
see also under individual
malady
hearth 25–6
heather 188
herbs
as charm 151
growth of 17
to clean air 207
herring 62
hoe 22
holly
as Christmas decoration 246
placed in coffin 143
protects against thunder
and lighting 17

thrashing chilblains with
   41
to protect house 18
Holy Innocents' Day 247
Holy Thursday 245
holy water
   bathing eyes with 211
   protects against ghosts
      and witchcraft 211
home
   avoiding fire in 19
   ax, bringing into 22
   baking bread in 19
   bees in 30
   birth in 24
   bluebottles in 30–1
   carrying a hoe into 22
   carrying a bride into 15
   cats in 16, 29–30
   coal, bread, salt, and
      a new broom 14
   cock crows and 21–2
   covering reflective surfaces
      during a storm 17
   death, opening windows
      and doors to aid soul
      after 20–1
   doors in 20–1
   fireplaces 25
   floor plan 14
   flowers and plants in 31
   flying creatures in 26–7
   gifts for new home owners 15
   hanging a kingfisher in
      to protect 17–18
   hearths 24–5
   horseshoes, hanging above
      a doorway for good
      luck 20
   keeping away witches from 18
   letting storm into 19
   locking out bad luck 16–17

mirrors and clocks 23–4
moving to a new 13–16
passing on the stairs 24
precautions indoors 23
salt in 24
spiders, rats and mice 29
storm protection 17–18, 19
taking eggs into 22
two people doing household
   chores together 26
vermin, warding off 19
visitors, signs of 21–2
walking into 22
honey 43
horses 172
horseshoe
   carrying for good luck 7, 194
   dropping into cream 214
   hanging up 20, 194, 214
keeps away fairies 151
houseleeks 16
hydrangeas 61

I
iron 215
   finding 193
   touching 213
   tools 214
   see also horseshoe
itchiness
   on ear 177
   on elbow 174–5
   on head 177
   on left palm 119
   on mouth 176
   on nose 176
   on right palm 118
ivy
   in the house 31
   grown on walls of house 18,
      145
   to divine future love 57

K
kingfisher 17–18
knives
   as a gift 23, 73
   dropping 22
   placed in cradle 113, 214
   sharpening after sunset 21
   using at Chinese New Year
      235
knotgrass 146

L
ladders 185
ladybugs
   landing on your hand 190
   seeing on an English farm 190
   sight of in France 190
   to divine future love 64–5
   to divine when and where
      marriage will take place 68–9
   wintering in your garage 190
lambs 91
laughter 174
lavender 13
left foot 22
lemon juice 38
letters 72
lilies 31
little people, magical
   see under individual name
lizard 41
love and romance
   apples and 54
   auspicious days 55–6, 58, 61
   bowls and 62
   candles and 60
   chestnuts and 66–7
   clover and 53
   cobwebs and 68
   dragon's blood and 66
   dreams and 57
   dumb cake and 59

eggs and 63–4

hair and 62–3

love letters 72

Midsummer Eve and 55–6, 64

moon and 62

omens 67–8

paper and ink and 58

petals and 67

plants and plums and 63

sage and 65

snails and 62

St. Agnes's Day Fast 61–2

St. Thomas's Eve 58

veils and 57

wraiths and 56–7

yarrow and 65

see also marriage and engagement

M

magpie

  bad luck for business 122

  good luck 122

  rhymes 170

mandrake 94

marriage and engagement

  bouquet 85

  breaking glass on 84

  chimney sweeps and 81

  choosing day of 68–9, 73–4, 75–6, 78

  color of wedding garments 77

  confetti, rice and 87

  engagement 74

  lovers' first meeting place 71–2

  moon and marriage day 86

  omens on 82–3

  orange blossom and 83

  pearls and 79–81

  photographs 73

  pins and 79

  rings 80

  shivaree and 87

  shoes 81–2

  sixpence and 74–5

  storks and 82

  veils and 79–80

  who will take control of 84, 86

May 94, 95, 108, 153, 169, 239, 240

May Day 94, 95, 108

May Eve 153

mice 40

Midsummer Eve 54, 55, 56, 58, 64, 95, 240

milk

  burning 125

  drinking ferret's 40

mirrors

  babies in 110

  breaking 23–4, 184

  brides and 23, 81

  turned or covered at time of death 143

mistletoe

  burning 93

  kissing under 92–3

  protects against thunder and lighting 17

moles

  feet 210

  front paw 210

  on the back of the neck 118

  under your left arm 118

molten lead 63

Monday 126

money

  bees and 125

  cats and 117–18

  clothes and 123

  coins see coins

  cuckoo calls and 116–17

  exams and 127

  finding 119–21

  fishermen and 124, 126–7

  itchy palms and 118–19

  spiders and 127–8

  sympathetic magic and 125

  sympathy cures and 115–16

  tea and 126

  transactions 122–4

monks and nuns, bad luck to meet 74, 172

moon

  asking to reveal your lover 62

  first kiss by light of 71

  looking through a handkerchief or reflected in water 69

  moving house and 13

moth 173

myrrh 147

N

needles

  dangling over pregnant woman's stomach 99

  dropping 22

  snapped 179

nettle 147

New Year 124, 231–5

New Year's Day 231, 232, 233, 234, 245

New Year's Eve 64, 146, 232

nose

  itch on 176

  nosebleeds 176

numbers

  counting 217–18

  double number 130–1

  odd 10, 131, 218–19, 225

  three 10, 101, 219, 220, 221, 224

  four 219, 221

  seven 222–3

  eight 224

nine 10, 224, 226

thirteen
   10, 90, 222, 225–7, 228–9

fourteen 228

666 221–2

nuts
  and babies 90, 93
  carrying a double nut 187
  eating both kernels of a double
    kernelled nut 90

O

omens
  appearance and 177–8
  at sea 174–5
  bread 182–3
  bugs 167–9
  candles and 183–4
  cats and 169, 171
  chairs and tables 183
  clairvoyants 180
  clothing and 179, 181
  cuckoos *see* cuckoos
  dogs and 171
  dreams and 181
  dropping, spilling, and
  breaking
    184
  drowning and 176
  ears and 177
  encounters and 172
  fingers and feet 178–9
  foals and 172
  hair and 178
  itching and 174–5
  ladders and 185
  laughter and 174
  magpies 170
  nose and 176–7
  plants 165
  predicting a visitor 173
  salt and 184

sieves 181–2

sky 166–7

stars 167

tickets and 173

weather 166

onions
  as a gift 15
  cutting in half and placed
    under bed 37
  grating and using as a mustard
    plaster 41
  medicinal use 207
  rubbing chilblains with 41
  spinning 62–3
  to divine future love 58

orpine, to divine future love
  64

P

Palm Sunday 17

paper and ink 58

parsley
  giving or receiving 165
  planting on Good Friday 244
  young women sow and pick
    94

patchwork quilt 73

pearls
  dreaming of 79
  wearing at a wedding 80
  as traditional wedding gifts
    80–1

photographs 73

picture
  falling from wall 184
  hanging above door or bed
    184

pigeon
  desire to eat 169
  plucking out heart, sticking
    pins in and placing under
    pillow 66

pigs
  bad luck for 73
  killing 91

pillows
  cases placed with their open
    ends facing out 243
  pigeon under 66
  wedding cake under 71

pine oil 40

pins 79

plants 63

pyramids 195

R

rabbits
  feet 190–1, 192
  saying three times on the first
    morning of each month
    197, 198

rain
  fallen on a tomb 38
  rainy days 13

rats
  charms to get rid of 203
  leaving boat 175
  leaving house 29

red thread
  catching troublesome spirits
    with 150
  to cure illness 205–6
  tied around cows tails to
    protect them from evil 35
  tying a sprig of rosemary
    inside a seashell with 147

rhymes
  gathering ivy and yarrow
    leaves and reciting 57
  magpie 170
  picking twig of ash and
    reciting 53
  reciting while tickling nose
    with yarrow 65

St. Agnes's Day fast rhyme 61
St. Thomas' Eve rhyme 58
to divine future station of lover
    63
to divine wedding day 68
to reignite lover's interest 66
ribbon/thread
    putting on a child 35
    tied around cows' tails 35
    tied to cradle or baby's
        underwear 35, 113
    wearing 47–8
rice 87, 95
rings
    as indication of love and
        marriage 80
    dangling over pregnant
        woman's stomach 99
    silver 212
robin
    seeing the first day of spring
        117
    seeing on Valentine's Day 236
rope
    hangman's 189, 213
    used to confine a troublesome
        spirit to its grave 146
rosemary
    to protect house 18
    tying a sprig inside a seashell
        147
rowan
    as charm against fairies 151
    hung over doorway 18, 145
    on a grave 201
    to protect ships 201
    to protect houses 201

S
sage
    couple plant 86
    used to divine future love 65

salt
    baby bathed in salt water
        100–1
    bringing into a new house 14
    helping someone to 25
    in boiled egg for St. Agnes's
        Day fast 61
    placed in baby's cradle 101
    spilling 184
    sprinkled on a doorstep
        after an unwelcome visitor
            has left 25
    sprinkling on baby teeth 109
    taking into a new house 25
    thrown on the doorstep after
        a beggar leaves 23
    thrown in fire 25
Saturday 69, 126, 181
scissors
    as a gift 23
    carrying 104
    dropping 22, 23
    falling 23
    using at Chinese New Year 235
shadows 140
shark's teeth 189, 197
sheep
    rubbing the inside of
        slaughtered skin 33
    skin placed on limbs of
        cramps sufferer 48
shoes
    on a table 23, 183
    placed in a T or cross shape
        48–9
    placed on windowsill 81
    silver placed in 212
    untied shoelaces 179
    wear and tear on 179
    wedding 81, 82, 212
shoulder bone 61
shrew 214

Shrove Tuesday 69, 246
sickness and health
    see health and sickness
silver
    coins in milkmaid's churn
        212
    collected at church 211–12
    in the sole of bridegroom's
        shoe 212
    rings help cramps 212
snail 62
snake
    as omen of death 29
    association with Satan 198
    putting skin in your wallet
        115
sneezing
    cats *see* cats
    sailors 175
    sayings after 47
Solstice, Winter 159
souls and spirits
    astral travel 136
    bee soul 133–4
    birds and 134–5
    blood and bone 133
    butterflies and 137
    candles and 145, 146
    channelling 138
    corpse eyes and 140
    cows and 136
    departing soul 140–2
    deterring spirits 139
    exorcism 138
    graveyards 144
    mirrors and 140
    pets and 135
    protecting home from
        145–6
    shadows and 139–40
    stars and 137
    suicides and 144

weather and 143
sparrow 236
spiders and spiderwebs
  enclosed in a reed and its
    grubs in a walnut shell 205
  in the house 127, 173
  in wedding dress 72
  kissing and 68
  landing on you 127
  to heal bleeding wound
    9–10, 45–6
  whirling around your head
    128
spitting 130, 133
spoon 23
sport 130–1
squirrel 236
St. Agnes's Eve 56, 59, 60,
  61–2
St. John's wort
  picking naked on
    Midsummer Eve 95
  planting 151
  using to ward off malevolent
    spirits 145, 201
St. Mark's Day 56–7
St. Mark's Eve 55, 56, 59, 60
St. Thomas's Eve 58
stairs
  carrying babies up 107
  passing on 24, 72
stars 99, 137
stockings
  putting on left leg first 48
  thrown at wedding 85
  wrinkled 67
stones
  hung around children's necks
    110
  hung in bedrooms 212
  hung in stables 212
  used to aide childbirth 49

storms, protection against 16–18
success and wealth see money
Sunday 37, 126, 243, 244
superstitions
  origins of 8–9
  science, philosophy and 7,
    9–10
  types of 10–11

T
tables
  placing objects on 23, 183
  three candles burning on 184
tea
  accidentally leaving the lid off
    a teapot while making 21, 173
  burning 126
  bubbles in 126
  finding a tea leaf or stalk
    floating in 21
  throwing away leaves 126
teeth
  baby teeth 108–9
  hanging a bag containing teeth
    around the neck 209–10
  large gap between 119
theaters 128–30
tickets 173
toads
  touching 34
  powdered 45
toadstones 210–11
toes 178
trees
  bringing boughs of into house
    90
  pear tree 247
  planting at front door 26
  predict the coming season 165
  poplar 71
  splitting and passing child
    through 41

Tuesdays 244
Twelfth Night 159

U
umbrella
  dropping 23
  open 23
  putting on a table 23, 183
urine 41

V
Valentine's Day 55, 56, 72,
  235–7
Valentine's Eve 58, 236
violets
  grown in and around house 145
  as symbol of fidelity 238

W
washing
  face in May dew 239, 240
  hands with another person 26
  laundry 245
water
  building house near 151
  crossing 40
  drawing first bucket from well
    232
  meeting near running 71
wealth see money
Wednesday 76, 244
whistling 11, 129
Whit Sunday 105
windows 20–1, 143, 232
wood 188
wool 207
wren's nest 33

Y
yarrow
  to cure nosebleeds 65
  to divine future love 57, 65